Good Lovers Make Great Parents

Good Lovers Make Great Parents

Pairing and Caring with Faith, Hope, and Love

Zane Alexander

BAKER BOOK HOUSE
Grand Rapids, Michigan 49516

ISBN: 0-8010-0217-6

Printed in the United States of America

Case histories described represent a composite of the author's clients and no one individual is portrayed in this book.

Chapter 9 "Love Communicates with Power" was first published as an article "Straight Talk About Talking with Teens" in *Survey* magazine, Atlanta, Georgia, September 1983. It was subsequently published by *Home Life* magazine, Nashville, Tennessee, March 1989 issue, and is used with permission.

The Revised Standard Version of the Bible is the primary source used in this book. Other versions used are King James Version (KJV), The New English Bible (NEB), and the Jerusalem Bible (JB).

To my parents

Theron Lee and **LaDell Alexander**

Contents

Preface

"Look both ways," my father said to me a hundred times in those early street-crossing days. It was good advice then. It is good advice now, especially for people crossing a street called *parenting*. Parenting is a dangerous street. More people are killed and maimed on it than on any other avenue of humankind. The street is not clearly marked and people drift upon it unexpectedly.

Parenting is a busy street. Many people travel it. Those who exit off the boulevard of marriage at an intersection called divorce, remain on the street of parenting. It is impossible to divorce one's kids. Those who find themselves off the street of parenting usually long for the day when they can get back on.

This is a book based on Christian concepts about traveling the roads of marriage and parenting. I believe that the apostle Paul wrote a road map for happy families in First Corinthians, chapter 13. He certainly did not intend to. Paul was not very excited about the streets of marriage or parenting. I doubt seriously if he ever traveled either, but the scribes of our sacred literature wrote more than they realized. The inspired Word teaches us more than those holy men probably intended to when they penned those sacred words of Scripture.

When Paul speaks of *hope*, he means anticipation for the apocalyptic return of our Lord Jesus Christ. When he talks about *faith*, he means commitment to Jesus Christ. But for the early Christians to exercise the experience of hope and the experience of faith, they had to take certain postures. I believe these same stances will make your marriage and parenting better. If you don't take them, my clinical experience indicates that your family will fail. These are the postures required to look both ways. Faith requires looking inward with personal commitment to your family. Hope requires looking outward to the community of the called, to the body of Christ, to the church. Only when you have looked both ways can you experience what Paul means by love. Love is learning to look both ways at the same time. Faith and hope are prerequisite to love. It takes commitment and community to make a family work.

This book is part inspirational and part instructive. This is both a Christian book and a parenting and marriage manual. The assumptions underneath the guidance and the hidden message in the numerous case studies are all based on the life and teachings of Jesus Christ.

Love alone is not enough. If you want to be happy traveling the street of parenting, you must have faith and hope also.

1

Parenting Prerequisites

The past two hundred years have been good for children, but bad for parents. A revolution has taken place. The children that were on the bottom of the pecking order have moved to the top, and parents who were on top, have moved to the bottom. There is a new problem in the hallways of family life. It is the mutiny of the kids. Two hundred years ago parents had such total control of their children that no one fantasized the kids might be a factor in marital break-ups. In the days prior to the Industrial Revolution, parents were monarchs and the children never revolted. In only two centuries the power of parents has decreased to the point that children exercise a decision-making role in the family. In my practice, I have seen nine-year-olds dictate to their mother how a five-year-old should be raised! Parents genuflect to their majesties, the children.

The advent of romanticism following the Industrial Revolution has been the precipitating cause. Before the Industrial

11

Revolution toddlers were placed in a big sock and hung on the wall. After the revolution, Dad went to the factory and Mom stayed home with the children. The toddlers were taken off the wall and Mom was driven up it. Child care improved with the birth of the nuclear family but Mom, until her recent return to the marketplace, was marooned in the lonely task of tending to children by herself. Many mothers still live a monastic life in which their only tasks are child care and housecleaning.

The human potential movement of recent years has further dethroned parents. It is open season on them. They are fair game. When parents are in the room, there is a free-fire zone. It is in vogue today to blame all of one's problems on defective parenting. "I just didn't get the fathering I needed," John says as he rationalizes away his responsibility for character flaws. The group-therapy movement has popularized this avenue of self-justification. The cacophony of this chorus has reached such proportions that today one wants to explode the rebuttal of Ezekiel, "Let it no more be said in Israel, the fathers have eaten sour grapes and the children's teeth are set on edge. The soul who sins, it shall die" (Ezek. 18:2–4).

Confidence

In light of these trends, it is not unusual for parents to have a loss of self-confidence. *Confidence is the first prerequisite for parenting.* Parents must be able to "walk on water," and they must know it. Their confidence in their ability to marshal meaning out of discordant family stress must be unshakable. As an orchestra conductor must be able to stare into fifty faces with the confidence he can turn them into a symphonic unity, so must parents look at their children with the assurance that they can change their chaotic confusion into functional family relationships.

How does one get confidence? It is self-taught. No one can jump off the ten-meter board for another person. One must take the plunge oneself. And your first child is not unlike jumping off the ten-meter board. The development of confidence is a natural process which comes from experience. Water flows downhill naturally, if there are no dams to prevent it. So it is with parental confidence. The goal of this book is to blow up the dams. I want to create an atmosphere where confidence can develop.

The first dam is the prevailing assumption that parents can only define themselves in relationship to their children. For years I answered the telephone "Dawn's Dad."

Consider a case study.

"Johnny put that gun down." Johnny is beating Cindy over the head with a sub-machine gun—a plastic play one—but it still hurts when it makes contact with her head.

No response from five-year-old Johnny who keeps banging away.

"Johnny, I said put that gun down, right now."

"She hit me first," he pauses long enough to lie, and then resumes his assault.

"Johnny, did you hear me?" Mother is getting red in the face. She is embarrassed by her total lack of control. She feels like picking up the little rascal and spanking him good, but she read a book somewhere that said not to do it.

By now, Cindy's mother has seen the assault and there follows the charge of the maternal brigade. The little girl's mother swoops up Cindy in her arms, sees the cut on her head, and glares at Johnny's mother. "You're going to have to do something about that kid of yours." No one knows this more than Johnny's mother. But no one tells her what to do. She pulls her little boy into the house and sulks until her husband comes home.

"What's the matter with you?" her husband interrogates on his entrance. The harried mother breaks into tears. The tired husband is impatient. He says he deserves a better welcome home and explodes. A quarrel becomes a fight. Johnny's dad storms out while Johnny's mother feels hurt, lonely, and desperate.

If this happens at your house, listen to some good news. Parents are people too! You have as much right to be on this planet as any cuddly, blue-eyed baby girl. Repeat this affirmation to yourself three times a day. Accept the fact that you are a human being too and that you have certain rights.

You have a right to an identity apart from your child. Notice in the story above, that it can be told without once naming the parents. If you suffer from a loss of identity, you need a parents' protection program.

Start your survival program *by refusing to "should" yourself to death.* Refuse to tell yourself that you ought to do such and such. For one week refuse to say or think the word *should*. If you catch yourself doing it, translate the should into a "want to" or "don't want to." Don't operate under the law which says you have to *earn* your right to be a parent. Operate under the law which says you have been *given* the right to be a parent. Insofar as possible, do what you want for one week. If you want to spank Johnny, spank him. If you don't want to clean the house, don't. If no one dies, loses a job, or leaves home, consider your new behavior acceptable.

Next, *refuse to set up any goal for yourself as a parent other than survival.* Take all of your "how to be a perfect parent" books, put them in a big pile in the front yard, douse them with lighter fluid, and burn them! Then stomp the ashes into the ground. Use the heels of your shoes and stomp hard. When Johnny says, "What's that for?" say, "Be quiet!" Your only goal is to survive one day at a time. Repeat this litany over and over, "I will not let Johnny drive me up the wall." The balance has been tilted in the favor of children for so long that parents are people without rights. You must assert your own rights, and your principal right is to survive.

For one week, talk in terms of what's good for parents, not what's good for children. Your words will guide your feelings. You can control your feelings by controlling your words. Talk about parents. Tell Robin (Cindy's mother), "Hey, we parents are people too. Why should we let ourselves be mistreated?" During this important first week you are better off if you limit your focus to one principle: Parents are people who have identity apart from their children.

If you don't have identity, you don't have control. You have anarchy. When anarchy results, parents become desperate. It is desperation that breeds child abuse. No parent has a right to abuse his or her child. But the solution to child abuse is not to lay a load of "shoulds" on the abusing parent.

A second dam on the river of confidence is the triumph of therapy at parental expense. In a well-known psychiatric clinic, I watched a video tape of one of their "success cases." Present at the counseling session were a twenty-eight-year-old female therapist, Mom and Dad who appeared to be in their midforties, and their eighteen-year-old daughter who had been a resident patient at the clinic for ten months. Mom and Dad drove in from out of town once a month for a family session. It was obvious from the start that the therapist was in alliance with the daughter, and that Mom and Dad would have to fend for themselves. Fifteen minutes into the session the daughter maliciously attacked her Mom. Dad was flabbergasted and remained mute most of the session. The therapist encouraged the daughter to continue. The daughter attacked both the character and integrity of her mother. The session ended with the daughter shouting and Mom sitting dejected and hurt and alone. Dad had even moved his chair away from her.

After the completion of the tape, the instructor stated that the daughter had made remarkable progress after this session and was released a few weeks later.

"What happened to her mom?" I asked.

"What do you mean?" the instructor hedged.

"You keep records on the entire family," I pointed out. "How did Mom do after the session?"

"I don't know," the instructor said. But confidence had left his voice, so I pursued the issue further. I later learned that the daughter was in the clinic by court order after having been caught selling drugs several times. She had made a small fortune in the drug business. Mom was devastated by the session and had been committed to the state mental hospital.

After the session, I remembered hearing an artillery officer say in Viet Nam, "I'm going to have to destroy that village in order to save it." The officer then ordered his Bravo battery to level the town with a 105 Howitzer barrage.

This is not an isolated incident. It has become acceptable for therapists to sacrifice parents to save the children. If parents believe they are responsible for all their children's mistakes, and if they believe they are expendable commodities in the marketplace of therapeutic intervention, a dam is erected on the river of confidence. I believe that parents aren't responsible for the whole litany of their children's sins. People err because people choose to err, and it isn't always their parents' fault. I also believe that it is heinous for a therapist to allow the destruction of any family member in a counseling session. "Let it no more be said in America: The fathers have eaten sour grapes and the children's teeth are set on edge. Children who traffic in drugs will suffer because of their own sin."

One of the biggest dams on the river is *the youth-centered culture that we allow to survive.* "You can't be too thin or too rich," is a popular saying in Atlanta. In the small rural village of Brighton, Tennessee, where I grew up, the townspeople would not have tolerated that saying two minutes. Being thin is an option many adults don't have. Since the adults decided what was beautiful in Brighton, thin was not in.

I was thin and suffered for it. "Boy, we're going to have to put some meat on your bones. Big gust of wind come along, why it would just blow you away." I had only one prayer, "Dear Lord, please let me gain some weight." It was an adult-centered community and the grown-ups carefully controlled the aesthetics of the community.

A youth-centered culture has produced child-centered families. In many families today children tell their parents how to raise their younger siblings. This causes a crisis for two reasons: Mom and Dad lose confidence when their parenting is judged harshly by their own children and, second, a child-centered family doesn't work. It is like a corporation where the janitors make executive decisions. Janitors are wonderful people but a company is in trouble if it is guided only by the judgment of the cleaning person. Children are wonderful, but a family is in trouble if children are playing a dominant role in the decision-making process. Parents must regain the throne room of decision making, even if it means they must swim against the current of a youth-centered culture. Confidence comes easy when you are on top.

A final dam on the river of confidence is a *lack of forgiveness.* You must forgive your parents. Failure to forgive them will drain you of confidence to parent your own children. To forgive them requires three steps. You must:

1. Articulate your anger in a safe setting with regard to their mistakes.
2. Realize they did the best they could.

3. Accept that when their best was not good enough, the deficit was unfortunate, but it was in no way "terrible."

Blowing up this dam, in my experience, is prerequisite for the development of confidence. Parents must turn inward to their family of origin. This inward focus must be one of forgiveness. I wasn't emotionally prepared to nurture my girls until I had forgiven my parents. Then I had confidence that regardless of my mistakes, the girls would mature into beautiful people. I also had the confidence that one day my girls would forgive me. My pilgrimage of forgiveness went like this.

Mother's Death

Strange how she was so sweet in death. Often she had been bitter in life—caustic, complaining, critical. All of this was gone now. She was dying and she knew it. The temporary misery of life had cleared away the underbrush of a relational jungle. When I entered the room, I felt the power of her faith touch the bare earth of my being.

"Well, here's Zane," she beamed when I touched her arm. I had never seen her smile so deeply. I had visited her only once in the previous year and felt guilty about my absence. I expected a touch of bitterness. There was none. She immediately removed a maze of life support tubes from about her head. "I can't see you with all this stuff they have wired to me."

My sister was aghast. "Mother don't. You may need that!"

"Don't worry. I'll be all right," she reassured. "This stuff makes the doctors feel better."

She did seem to be all right. It had been ten years since she had seen my sister and me at the same time. She reacted as if we lived down the road and were devoted children. We weren't. My mother had left when I was thirteen and Joyce nine. For thirty years my sister and I had seen her, at most, once a year and rarely were we able to plan a trip together.

I tried hard not to cry. I tried hard to talk. I succeeded in neither. I didn't know what to say. Joyce did better. I held Mother's hand while Joyce made small talk. Mother seemed satisfied. I touched and Joyce talked. It was supposed to be different. I was the therapist, and Joyce the mother. Death reversed our roles and made us humble before its awesome power.

I remembered a crisp October morning in West Tennessee. Mother and I sat on the living-room couch, and she confessed for the first time that she was leaving my father. I begged her not to go. Here in Dallas I wanted to beg her again, but it seemed as futile now as it did then. Mother was going, but this time she was doing it differently. This time she was saying good-bye and doing it pleasantly.

"We love you," she said to Joyce and me. We knew the first person singular was far beyond her power to say. We were grateful for the first person plural. Mother did not express love directly. She had told me about my breech birth and how worried she had been when the doctor said there wasn't much hope the baby would live. "I was so happy when I heard you cry," she told me. There had been indirect expressions of love, but this was different. It was direct and unencumbered with qualifying adverbs.

When Joyce and I turned to leave her bed in the big intensive care ward, she looked directly at me and said, "Hon, don't forget to close the door."

I didn't know what she meant, but I replied, "Sure, Mother, I'll close the door." There wasn't any door to close. Mother was somewhere else. Perhaps she was in the parsonage in Tennessee, where the winters were bitter cold; perhaps in North Dallas where she grew up. I didn't know and I dared not ask.

I like to think that she spoke more than she said. I like to think that she urged me to close the door on a difficult childhood, to close the door on my bitterness about the divorce, to close the door on my guilt and anger. I had long known that only when I closed these doors could I open the door to forgiveness.

Mother died a few days later. I never saw her conscious again. But it was okay. She had said good-bye, and she did it with grace.

Confidence to parent your children will develop as naturally as water running downhill. But if there are dams, the river of confidence will be impeded. The biggest dam is built when you fail to forgive your parents. In the process of parenting we want to give our children "roots and wings." We want them to have the roots of our value systems and the wings of autonomy. We want them to be grounded in our faith and yet free to fly their own course in life. But you cannot give what you do not have. One must have freedom to give freedom. The only way to get freedom is to forgive your parents.

Control

The second prerequisite for parenting is *control.* You must be able to control your children. You can't operate unless you control your operating room. Parents must have sufficient ego strength to marshall their resources and to structure their family settings. You must realize that what you are doing is open-heart surgery. Tolerate no disrespect in your operating suite.

Parents are better off if they can control what happens when their children enter the room. Children start the day intent on training their parents to do what they want. Their little feet hit the floor with one agenda: How can we manipulate Mom today? Their plan of operations is to seize control by breakfast. If they do, the war is over and anarchy reigns.

Even when the kids are miserable, they are reluctant to surrender their game plan. Parents must learn to monitor parent-child communication to the extent they can recognize what is happening and control it. The parent must be the quarterback. If the parents don't call the plays, the kids will.

People with low ego strength are better off not having children. Passive people will not enjoy the parenting process. They are subject to the manipulations of their children to a greater degree than are dominant people. Parenting is hard enough for the strong-willed and the stout-hearted; it can be total frustration for the passive. When one steps into the lion's den of parenting, one had best be a lion tamer.

If parents are dominant by nature, really believe they can "walk on water," and know what they want to happen, they are in a better posture to take control. No one will hand you control. You must seize it, and you can't always be nice in the process. The issue is who makes the rules in your family. This is a war you must win. If you lose it, you will sacrifice the whole process of parenting.

Often in this war of wills it is helpful to learn to identify what your children are pulling from you. If your children are pushing against you in order to pull rejection from you, you must be able to identify the process and refuse to cooperate. Kids don't always pull love from their parents. Your teddy-bear kids will, but all kids are not born teddy bears. (This is discussed in a later chapter.) Some children are born re-bellious. The challenge of parenting is to give these children room in which to rebel, but to realize that all rooms must have walls. It is a parental task not only to build walls but also to reinforce them to withstand the gale-force fury of a youth-centered culture.

Control is largely an issue of bottom lines and boundaries. If both are firm and enforced, you will have control. In the routine process of parenting boundary setting is a pivotal issue. If it is done well, control is axiomatic. If it is not done well, anarchy is certain. Boundary setting is second only to physical sustenance in the priority of parental respon-sibilities. The issue is not whether or not to set boundaries. The issue is how to go about it.

Step one in boundary setting: *be sure your boundaries are reasonable.* If you require your children to come in at six o'clock on a summer night when the other kids on the block can stay out till eight, you've got a lot of explaining to do. Just because your mother made you come in at six o'clock twenty-five years ago is not, in and of itself, justification for you to establish the same boundary with your children. Rea-sonable means what is necessary for the health, security, and happiness of children in the time and place where they live. Most unreasonable boundaries result from living in the past.

Step two: *limit your boundary setting.* Many parents set so many boundaries it is impossible to enforce all of them. You are better off not to have a boundary than to have one which you cannot patrol. An example is, "Brush your teeth before you go to bed." It is impossible to tell if teeth have been brushed. You are better off not to have the rule than to be forced into, "Did your sister brush her teeth?" Unenforceable rules pull parents into Gestapo tactics.

Establish no boundary unless you have the time and en-ergy to enforce it. When rules are broken without con-sequence, your control is eroded. You don't lose control of your children in some apocalyptic temper tantrum; your power base is slowly eroded with each unenforced rule. Con-trol slips away from you slowly.

Step three: *defend your boundaries with your life.* If you draw a line and your child puts his toe across it, you have war. And it is a war which you must win. How do you win the war? Discipline! Which kind of discipline depends on which kind of kid you have. There are four kinds: *straight arrows*, *teddy bears*, *little scientists*, and *rompers*. In a later chapter you'll learn how to tell the type of your child and which discipline works best, but the principle is: "Children must have a reason to regret their transgression." (from Samuel Butler, "Spare the Rod and Spoil the Child," seventeenth century. Proverbs 13:24, "He who spares the rod hates his son, but he who loves him is diligent to discipline him.")

Step four: *expect the boundaries to be tested.* Children define who they are as people by pushing against boundaries. When they test a boundary and find it firm, they feel secure. Don't expect your kids to express gratitude for this security. Expect them to grumble and groan. An old army saying is "When the troops are happy, they will complain a lot. If they stop complaining, expect trouble." Children will complain about boundaries: "No one else has to . . ." is a litany of childhood. If your children push against a boundary and it collapses, they will feel insecure. Indeed, they *will* be insecure. Don't let it happen.

Step five: *tolerate no disrespect as a boundary setter.* Everyday while conducting therapy I say to some parent, "Are you going to let him get away with that disrespect?" Children need space in which to ventilate anger, but this can be done without disrespect. A child can say, "I'm angry." "This isn't fair." "I don't like this," or even "I hate you," without conveying disrespect, but once the sentence begins with the second person pronoun *you*, there is a danger of disrespect.

"You aren't fair."

"You don't care about me."

"You like Susie better than me."

"You just want to ruin my life."

These sentences are judgmental, oversimplified and presumptive. They presume that your child can get inside you and determine what your inner feelings are. This is disrespect. Don't tolerate it.

Disrespect can be communicated in action as well as words. I don't necessarily consider a teenager stomping off to her room and slamming her door as disrespectful. This particular activity could be framed as normal ventilation of anger, if the parent had completed the transaction. But if a child destroys another person's property or injures someone, this activity must be interpreted as disrespect.

A seven-year-old was tearing up merchandise in a department store. He was throwing anything he could reach on the floor. Two salespeople told him to stop. "Listen, young man. That isn't nice." A hair dryer went crashing to the floor.

"If you don't stop we're going to find your mother and tell her what you're doing." The kid smiled, grabbed a bottle of hair spray and threw it at the woman who chided him. In desperation the women looked for help. They saw a family therapist whom they knew and pleaded for help.

The therapist said he would be glad to speak to the child. He bent over and whispered in the kid's ear. The seven-year-old paused a second, looked to his left, and shot out of the store.

The salespeople turned to the therapist. "What did you say to him?"

"I told him that if he didn't get out of here, I was going to beat him up."

When setting boundaries and bottom lines, tolerate no disrespect in word or deed. Rearing children is unmitigated joy when parents have control; when parents don't have control, the whole process of parenting breaks down. You cannot parent without control. Without control the best you can do is to provide custodial service. With control rearing children is fun. Many people have struggled for so long in the anarchy of permissiveness, they cannot imagine the pure pleasure of parenting. The abnormal has become normal for them. If this is true, you will need professional help to normalize the situation.

Bottom Lines

A bottom line is a nonnegotiable boundary. It grows out of a parent's system of values. A bottom line is a behavior that a parent will tolerate under no conditions. It may or may not involve violence. It may or may not involve drugs—but it is always an issue that threatens to destroy the process of parenting itself.

Every parent should list his or her bottom lines. Ask yourself what are the child behaviors that you are totally intolerant of. You must be exceedingly explicit. An example: "I will not tolerate the use of illegal drugs in my house or on my property at any time." Your bottom lines must be enforceable. "Don't use drugs" is unenforceable. There is no way you can patrol your child's behavior twenty-four hours a day.

Every parent needs a support system to enforce bottom lines. The acting-out behavior of teenagers is so entrenched in our youth-centered culture that it is futile for a parent to announce a bottom line without having a group of people to give guidance and emotional support in the enforcement of it. List your bottom lines on the left side of a sheet of paper. On the right side, opposite each entry, list the support group that will help you enforce the bottom line. If you don't have a support group, forget bottom lines.

At the top of the page, write: BEHAVIOR THAT I AM TOTALLY INTOLERANT OF. Try not to list more than three or four. It is hard to find enough support groups. TOUGH LOVE is the best known such group. Every counseling center has therapy groups. Your church may have support groups for parents. If they don't, scream like one possessed until they get one. It is unconscionable for a church today not to have a parent-support group. The fact that churches frequently have youth ministers, but seldom have a minister to parents or a minister to families indicates the pervasiveness of our youth-centered culture.

Once your list is complete, discuss it with your support group. Pay close attention to your course of action if the bottom line is broken. Know exactly what you will do and who will help you. Be certain you can follow through with the consequences. If your bottom line is: I will call the police if my child assaults me again, be sure you can do it. Be prepared to see your teenager go to jail. Work through any guilt feelings in advance with your group.

If you cannot find a group or if the group experience doesn't satisfy you, make an appointment with a family therapist. Look for one in the yellow pages under: *Marriage and Family Counselors.* Call a therapist who is a member of the American Association for Marriage and Family Therapy. Few other professionals are trained to help you with this kind of family problem.

Balance

Parenting requires balance. Think of balance as the ability to paint with more than one color. Parenting is not monochromatic. It requires people to have many pigments on their palettes. The artistry of parenting is found in the broad repertoire of human interactions that people have at their command. Parents can comfort, support, teach, reflect, confront, clarify, and empathize. They can laugh, learn, grieve, and rejoice. They are refreshingly real, because their balance provides them a broad range of responses. They are not preprogrammed as tradition would have them be. Their eclecticism deepens their well of resources. They break new ground with every parent-child encounter. Parenting is also like jazz. It improvises on a hundred themes, and great parents write their own themes. Many themes are used only once. As a brilliant comet on a dark, desert night, they illuminate a trackless expanse of sand, only to disappear over the horizon seen by no one except parent and child. There is no greater art form.

Balance can be taught but not in a weekend workshop. To really comfort, parents must have a broad overview of human institutions, and the development of this perspective takes time.

Reflecting seems simple, but it is an art within itself. To do it properly requires consummate skill.

The blind cannot lead the blind—at least not well. Parents will be profound teachers, but they can no more teach what they don't know than they can come from where they haven't been. Parents teach human relationships, and this is a far-ranging field of knowledge. Their internship in the school of hard knocks must be extensive.

Parenting requires that confrontation be done in kindness and for the benefit of the child, not for the benefit of the parent. This kind of confrontation is harder to learn than the blatant bumping that hostile people pass off as encounter.

To give empathy requires an active imagination, a posture of caring, and a wide range of experiences. Parents empathize with their children. Empathy is different from sympathy. Sympathy is giving pity: "Oh, you poor thing." The communication of pity will make children feel worse. If there is an excessive expression of pity, the child can be driven to suicide. Empathy is emotional togetherness between parent and child.

Yes, parenting requires balance. One can't be a guide in

the tropic jungle of human relationships unless one's experience is broad and one's imagination is deep. When clients describe bad parents to me, they often use one adjective. Their parents may have been critical, nonnurturing, absent, but they are usually described in one word. Bad parents don't have balance.

Timing

Timing is totally intuitive. Parenting is more than assembling pigments; it is also applying each one at the right moment. It is that spontaneous reflex action of a parent that seizes a particle of time and maximizes every ounce of it.

Timing can be improved by training and instruction but it cannot be created. The germ of genius must be there.

Fifty years ago when extended families were the norm, a parent could turn to a grandparent who lived in the house and say, "Did I come down too hard on the kid?"

"I don't think you were too hard. It might have been better to do it after supper up in his room," Grandfather might say. Fifty years ago there were other adults close by who could serve as guides in correcting timing errors.

All of these people are gone. None of them live in the same house with Jane and John. Today parents must turn to another source to find correction for their timing errors.

Group therapy provides one of the best settings in which to improve one's timing. In group, timing errors are more easily seen and more readily corrected. People often don't become parents until they have served an apprenticeship in some kind of group experience.

In the Greek language there are two words for time, *chronos* from which there are many derivatives and *kairos* from which there are no derivatives. *Chronos* is tick-tock time. It is quantitative and refers only to a passage of time. *Kairos,* however, refers to the critical moment. (For example, Mark 1:15: "The time is fulfilled and the kingdom of God is at hand.") It is the time of harvest when the crops must be brought in or perish in the fields; it is the time of childbirth when the baby must be delivered, or both the baby and the mother die; it is the time of battle when the decisive maneuver must be made or the war is lost. It is qualitive and critical. Parents are masters of *kairos*. They have a peculiar genius to recognize the critical moment and to revel in it.

Practice Economy

My approach to parenting places less emphasis on communication than do others, but since so much is being said about parent-child communication, I want to deal with the subject. Here is a case study in point.

Josiah Jones was an intense twenty-seven-year-old-high-school teacher. In college he majored in psychology and determined that he was going to communicate with his kids better than his parents had with him. He was a supernice guy, proud of his patience with his four-year-old and secretly intolerant of parents who hollered at their children.

Edison was an overactive four-year-old. To him couches and beds were trampolines to bounce on. A typical conversation between father and son went like this, "Son, would you take your feet off the couch? When you rub your dirty shoes on the couch, mud rubs off on it, and daddy has to clean it all up."

"I don't want to."

"Edison, I really don't have time to clean the couch again. Please take your feet off."

"No."

"Son, do you want your daddy to have to work on the couch all the time? That's time I don't have to play with you."

No response from Edison and no removal of the muddy shoes. This exercise in futility would go on for hours. Josiah Jones would so exhaust himself trying to communicate with his four-year-old that he had little energy left to talk to his wife. He was calm with his kid but negligent with his wife.

"Why don't you just spank him," she would say.

"I don't believe in punishment; I can discipline Edison without resorting to that," Josiah would answer.

"You know he takes advantage of you."

"Nonsense."

"Honey, it's obvious. The kid has you wrapped around his little finger."

"I don't need anybody to tell me how to raise my boy."

"The kid is spoiled rotten."

"I don't want to talk about it," Josiah would declare. They didn't. They didn't talk about anything the rest of the day.

Josiah's mistake was a total disregard for economy. He wanted Edison's feet off the couch. To express this idea he used over thirty words when a forceful communication of six words, "Get your feet off the couch," would have been better. When this one experience is multiplied by a long day of parenting, the waste of energy is exorbitant. This energy loss cost Josiah his marriage. His burning desire to be "a good parent" was so consuming that he sacrificed his marriage in the process. A lack of control in parent-child relationships can cause a communication nightmare.

Touch

Kids need to be touched. They need to be touched a lot, especially kids twelve and younger. If they don't get positive touching, they will act out to get negative touching. Spanking is better than no touching, but spanking is not as good as hugging. The more you touch your children physically, the more warmth and love you give them. A bumper sticker in California reads: 76 HUGS A DAY WILL KEEP THE THERAPIST AWAY.

Susan Johnson was raised in a family where there was little physical expression of love—there was little physical expression of anything. Her father was a strong-willed Puritan type. He never failed to exercise control. Susan always knew where the boundaries were, and it was also clear what would happen if she transgressed these boundaries. At least it was clear in principle. In reality Susan seldom tested these boundaries. She could not remember getting a spanking, nor could she remember disobeying her parents.

There was no lack of control in her upbringing. Susan had enormous stability in her childhood, but there was no touching, and there was little warmth. Her parents lived in a rural community in North Carolina, where most people believed that dancing was wrong. They never really said why dancing was wrong. When some college kids would press the adults for an answer, they would say something about the physical touching involved and that it would invariably lead to other things. No one asked what the other things were; everyone knew the awful consequences were *sex.*

Susan never really questioned all of this until her own children were growing up. They threw temper tantrums, even though she spanked them vigorously. Susan was desperate when a neighbor suggested that she might have to spank them less if she hugged them more. Susan tried it, and it worked! She not only survived her kids; she also saved her marriage.

Jeff, her husband, had complained for years about her lack of affection for him. After practicing on the kids, she learned how to hug her husband—even in the front yard. She knew that her father would "roll over in his grave" if he knew about such scandalous behavior, but so be it. Dad was dead.

If physical touching is hard for you, start by wrestling with your young children. Roll over and over with them on your living-room floor. They will love it, and you will too. Let them push against you as they assert themselves. This will help them in ways we don't yet understand. I wrestled with my youngest daughter when she was six and seven. Every evening after supper, I would get on my knees in the living room; we would interlock fingers and push against each other. Sometimes I would push her back against the couch but more often than not, I would let her push me down on the floor. I would fall prone on my side. She would then pounce on top of me and try "for all she was worth" to keep me from getting up. She quickly learned that if she could pin my arm, it would be difficult for me to get up. She would grip my wrist with both her hands and struggle to hold it out from my body. She also learned that if she spread her feet apart, she had more leverage.

Dawn and I would talk constantly during these "wrestling matches."

"I'm going to get you good," she would assert.

"No fair doing your hardest," I would protest. (This would guarantee that she would do her hardest.)

"If I get up from here, I'm going to get you good," I would tease. Then, when I was about halfway up, she would spread her feet and push me back down.

"No fair doing your hardest," she would grunt.

She is a young woman now, and we haven't wrestled since the second grade, but we have a warm, loving relationship in which there is much hand holding and hugging.

When your kids become teenagers, they may want less touching. They are beginning to pull away, to untie the apron strings, and it is important for you to respect their wishes. But if there has been touching before adolescence, there will be touching after adolescence. After their rebellion, they will come back.

Part **1**

Parenting
by Faith

2

Go Beyond Communication to Commitment

Low is one saved?" the teenager wanted to know. The question had an academic tone to it. The teenager is asking for information. He is acutely interested in what is right and wrong. He is curious about the "after life" and deeply worried that doing "wrong things" will result in an apocalyptic "trip to the principal's office" or something worse. The teenager doesn't like the feeling of being caught, and going to hell is the ultimate caught.

Mom doesn't like the feeling of being put on the spot. Being "put on the spot" means being asked questions that have no clear-cut answers. Mom is prepared. She has memorized nine succinct answers to nine serious questions. The first on her list is: "How is one saved?" The teenager's tone was academic, but he was not nearly so pedantic in his question as Mrs. Jones is in her answer.

"John, the Bible says to be saved you have to have faith."

"What does that mean?" the teenager pursues in a tone less intellectual.

Mrs. Jones becomes more desperate and less wordy. "Believe in Jesus Christ."

"I believe that Jesus lived and died and was raised from the dead. Is that it?" the teenager wants to know.

"That's it," Mom says. "But it's important to realize what the Bible says about. . . ." Mrs. Jones is off and running about some issue less ambiguous and more dear to a mother's heart. And there are a bunch: drinking, drugs, teenage sex, disrespect to parents, and on and on.

But there is no issue more important to seventeen-year-old John than that of faith. He knows that faith is somehow connected to being saved, and he has an unarticulated hunch that it is also connected to being married. Being saved in the next life and being married in this life are both important to John.

Mrs. Jones has failed to help John on either issue. She implies that faith is a matter of giving intellectual assent to the facts of Jesus' life. John knows it is really more than that, but he doesn't know the questions to ask.

The noun *faith* and the verb *believe* are the same word in the original Greek of the New Testament. The noun is *pistis* and the verb is *pisteuo*. They both mean commitment. John needs to know that the process of "being saved" is related to the process of committing one's life to Jesus Christ. Faith is not the content of one's intellectual inventory of religious ideas. Faith is a process of commitment.

One purpose of this book is to say that parenting is a process of commitment. The process is one of faith, and faith *is* commitment. For the Christian, the ultimate faith posture is commitment to the Father of our Lord Jesus Christ. My experience in the practice of therapy is that a similar (if less total) commitment to one's spouse and children is necessary for a family to work.

Romantic love is not enough. This kind of love is a delightful set of delusions shared by two people both of whom have recently had a psychotic break. Romantic love is wonderful, exciting, but the emotional intoxication will not last. Romantic love is a delicious excursion into temporary insanity. Insanity is a legal term. It means a distortion of time, place, and person. The insane person doesn't know when, where, or who he is. This is an apt description of someone who has "fallen in love." But it won't last. *Love alone is not enough.*

Faith also is required. Romantic love is an exercise in feelings. Feelings are fickle. Faith is firm. If John and Jane are to have a functional marriage—one that works—they must go beyond feelings to commitment. They must make a firm decision to live together regardless of the gale-force winds of emotion which pummel the bridge of their marital bond.

Faith in marriage is a firm decision that the quest is over. Single people search. They search for the "right" person to marry. This search may monopolize much of their waking existence. Every social function is evaluated by its potential to produce the "right" person. In a romanticized culture, the supreme act of faith is getting married. Jane and John expect each other to meet most of their human and emotional needs. They know that if they are not "right" for each other, many of their needs are not going to be met. They take the search seriously.

Faith means that the search is over. Usually the conscious mind will accept the end of the quest before the unconscious mind does. The hidden recesses of the unconscious mind

may not attend the wedding. It pouts in a protracted celi-
bacy, or it lingers in a previous marital commitment. The
unconscious mind accepts the new relationship—if at all—
very slowly. It has a will of its own. One must wait on the
unconscious, like one waits on the Spirit of God. In the
center of their souls, Jane and John may continue the quest
long after they are legally married. But there must come a
time when even the unconscious mind accepts the finality of
the marital event.

When this time comes, it will be an act of faith. And the
act will be more process than content. It won't be any single
deed done, but rather it will be a process of committing
oneself to a life partner. Faith is acting as if the right person
is found when all the evidence is not yet in. "Faith . . . makes
us certain of realities we do not see" (Heb. 11:1 NEB).

In a second marriage, faith is also the assurance that the
unfinished business of the first marriage is over. Some
therapists say it takes five years to get over a bad marriage.
I've found that people who work hard in therapy can take
care of the loose ends of their previous marriage in less time
than that. But the fact remains that a failed marriage is a
broken commitment, and one cannot overcome this kind of
failure without a tremendous exercise of faith. Jane and
John will dream about their ex-spouses, and these dreams
will be bad. Faith is the assurance that the nocturnal remembrance of past commitments will not destroy the sacred
content of the present bond.

Commitment isn't popular today. *Communication* is the
shrine at which Americans have worshiped for the last ten
years. Unfortunately, the god of communication doesn't deliver. Its high priests promise a panacea of healed relationships and repaired marriages. Each priest has his own
twist to improving communication and his own eightfold

path to the promised land of marital bliss. Like patent medicines of the last century, they offer placebos at best and false hope at worst.

Why? Why will decent people and good writers overemphasize communication? First, *it is easy to sell.* There is little risk. Who could question the value of learning to express your feelings better? It is easy to sell because people are lonely and locked inside of themselves. They desperately want to break out. Communication is the key, we are told, to opening the door to a new and exciting world of meaningful relationships. Would that it were true! Unfortunately human relationships don't unfold so easily.

Second, *communications are easy to teach.* Unlike other human disciplines, the art of talking can be reduced to ten easy steps which most people can learn. Many counselors have been influenced by the medical model which prefers a neat orderly world where you take a pill after meals and once again before bedtime. Communication theories lend themselves to a mechanistic format. They can be taught "by the numbers."

Third, *improved communications give quick results.* You can upset the normal routine of relationships at your house by learning some communication "tricks." It's an easy way to achieve a momentary victory. You can get a quick surge of power and the feeling is exhilarating. But when the dust settles and your children have recovered from the shock of your "new thing," your parenting will drift back to its past stagnant state. And you will be more depressed than ever. There is no magic in talking.

Most people communicate better than they think they do. My clinical experience is that parents may have difficulty in putting their feelings into words, but family members seldom lack knowledge about what each other feels. They assume their inability to articulate their feelings means they can't communicate. Nonsense! Your every physical move is communicating what is going on inside you. It is really not ignorance of your children's feelings that destroys your parenting; it is more a matter of two sets of feelings being on a collision course.

I have listened to operas for years, most of which are sung in languages I don't know. I don't know the words, but the power of the composer to communicate with me is not limited by language. If this can be true between me and a musician I never met, how much more can we communicate with a family member who shares the same dwelling with us. Words aren't all-important to communication.

I have also found that many people can write their feelings better than they can speak them. I am a dominant person, growing up with three younger sisters. I was the son of a rural Baptist minister who ran with total control the small town where I lived. My dominance came naturally, and this has not made it easy for others to articulate negative feelings to me. They have, however, been able to write down their anger and frustration. My clinical experience indicates that most family members can communicate one way or the other, but communication, in and of itself, cures nothing!

It can make matters worse. There are bad communication techniques that can destroy your family. The first of these is the analytical. This approach to communications teaches you how to analyze what is going on between people when they talk. The first assumption is that if you "know" what is happening in the communication, you are better off. The second assumption is that by using analytical techniques you can *really* know. I challenge both assumptions. Human relations are so intrinsically complex that no one technique can begin to fathom what is going on down deep.

Second, knowledge which comes from a process of labeling has little power to change behavior. Being able to name something or to label something doesn't mean that one can understand it or control it. What is most damaging is that analyzing the transaction requires you to act like an authority. Acting like an authority in the quagmire of a communication failure is ludicrous. When your children stop laughing, it won't be funny.

No one likes to be analyzed by a family member. It is putting yourself in a one-up position while putting your children in a one-down position. At first it may have the excitement of any new game, but when the new wears off, you and your family will be more desperate than ever.

The bombastic techniques of communication are equally damaging. The best known of these is Gestalt Therapy. It claims to be more than a communication technique but, in my experience (and that of my clients), the most important focus is on communication. Gestalt Therapy teaches you how to explode your feelings. The "really together" person (*gestalt* is German for "whole") should be able to explode feelings of joy, grief, orgasm, and anger. In family life the explosion of anger is sometimes damaging. If the anger is rational, reasonable, and focused, the explosion of it can be a positive experience, provided the explosion is within the bounds of what the culture will accept. Unfortunately Gestalt Therapy is not aware of these limitations, and people are taught to explode *all* of their feelings.

The end result is an emotional fire fight in which family members throw hand grenades at each other. Hand grenades hurt. They also damage the superstructure of the family relationship. An emotional orgy is not good communications. At least it is not good for your family life.

Nat and Julie

Nathaniel Hawthorne Jones was long, lean, and super-intense. He was twenty-seven and according to his therapist, "tied up in knots." When he was angry, the muscles in his face would visibly quiver. When he sat, his right leg was constantly moving. His heel moved back and forth, pivoting on the ball of his foot, as if it wanted to break away from the rest of his body.

Nat worked hard. He was addicted to his job in personnel and secretly intolerant of anyone who did not share his addiction.

Julie Jones was eight inches shorter than her six-foot-two-inch husband. She felt dwarflike in his presence. She was a pleasant and attractive person but somewhat sickly—yet, somehow, she managed to hold her own with Nat when they quarreled. He sometimes complained about her doctor bills.

"I can't help it—I'm sick," Julie said one afternoon when Nat was upset.

"Sure, you can," her husband disagreed.

"You think I get sick on purpose?"

"I don't know what you do on purpose, but I think you go to the doctor to get attention and not to get well."

"Nathaniel Jones! How dare you imply I'm not really sick. You're not perfect either, you know."

"What do you mean?"

"I mean that you're tense and high-strung, because you want to be that way," Julie explained.

"I was born this way," Nat rebutted.

"I don't believe you," Julie said. "If you would see a counselor, he'd tell you the same thing."

"We can't afford a counselor. It's all I can do to pay your doctor bills."

"Of course we can. Maybe I wouldn't have to see the doctor so much, if you weren't so uptight all the time."

"So it's my fault you're sick," Nat shot back.

"Not really, but I do want you to talk to someone. You work hard all day, and you know that you do more than your share at the office. It might help to unwind with someone other than me," Julie said with a snugly tone.

"Well, I'll think about it."

Two weeks later Nat was more nervous than usual and decided he would see a counselor. The counselor was supportive and yet confrontive with Nat. He taught Nat a bombastic mode of communications. Within six weeks Nat was good at exploding his feelings, especially his anger. He and the counselor would shout at each other.

The counselor could take it, but Julie couldn't. "I'm really angry at you," Nat screamed his third week into counseling. He spit the words out with such velocity that Julie recoiled. She backed halfway across the kitchen, terrified that he was going to hit her.

"Please, Nat, don't scream."

"I'll scream if I want to scream," he shouted even louder.

Julie ran out of the kitchen with Nat at her heels. "Don't you run out on me," he bellowed behind her.

"Nat, please, please."

"Don't you 'please' me," Nat's eyes bulged with his wrath. Julie was terrified. She did not say another word. She curled up on the couch in a prenatal position and cried. Nat slammed the living-room door behind him as he charged out.

This experience recurred on a weekly basis for three months. Then Julie left. The following year they were divorced. Nat's new-found power in his ability to explode his anger so overpowered his wife that the balance of their relationship was destroyed, and their marriage was over. If your anger is irrational, the explosion of it will only breed more anger, and the nuclear reaction will devastate your intimate relationships.

How can you tell when your anger is rational? Albert Ellis and Robert A. Harper have performed a monumental service to human relationships with the Rational Emotive Therapy

(RET). In *A New Guide to Rational Living* (Wilshire, 1975), Ellis teaches the ABC Syndrome in human experience. The response at *C* is not caused by the stimulus at *A*. What your spouse does or doesn't do isn't really what makes you angry. "My husband is driving me up the wall," Jane will say. But her husband's behavior is *A* and her response is *C* and *A* doesn't cause *C*. *B* causes *C* and *B* is your belief systems. *B* is how you interpret *A*. What drives Jane up the wall is how she interprets her husband's behavior. If she uses irrational words, such as "awful, terrible, disgraceful" to describe her husband's behavior, her anger will be irrational.

Her husband's behavior may be unpleasant, inappropriate, unfortunate, but it is not likely to be awful or terrible. The more Jane tells herself irrational things, the angrier she becomes, and the less chance her marriage has of surviving. The communication of irrational feeling will destroy the bridge of your marriage.

If you shouldn't communicate some of your feelings, what should you do with them? A quick answer is to therapeutically remove them. By simply reading Ellis's books, I have been able to remove much of the anger I directed toward others. When I'm angry, I remind myself that what someone has done or not done isn't awful; it isn't terrible and although it may be unpleasant, my angry feeling should be kept in proper perspective. I also ask myself, "Who am I to demand that everything others do or don't do should please me? Who am I to demand that the future not intrude on my present with anything that I haven't enjoyed in my past?" We are prone to err, and it is not rational to expect our children to be otherwise. I have learned to be cautious in the communication of my anger. When I feel angry, I do more talking to myself than to my children. It is better to work your anger out than to talk it out. *There is no magic in talking.*

If you want to improve your communication, the best technique is one developed in California by Ted Crawford. He called it Revolving Discussion Sequence (RDS). It is a structured sequential method in which people revolve roles. Thousands of people have improved their communication using RDS.

It is a three-step process, and it requires considerable discipline on the part of family members. It should not be attempted when you are emotionally upset or when you are physically tired. You should set aside an hour when you are reasonably refreshed and will not be disturbed. Step one is called "Statement." Person A (Jane) makes a statement to Person B (John). The statement must be on one topic and should be no longer than one paragraph (six or seven sentences). When Person A has completed the statement, he or she will say, "End of Statement," or words to this effect. It takes considerable practice to learn to make a good statement.

Step two is "Understanding." John will repeat back to Jane the statement just made. "Jane, I hear you saying. . . ." John can give understanding in one of three ways: (1) repeat back the words of the statement verbatim; (2) paraphrase the words of the statement; or (3) give an illustration that reflects back the meaning of the statement. The third alternative is difficult and should not be tried until you have gained considerable expertise in this technique. The verbatim and the paraphrase are the best ways to give understanding when you are new at RDS. The rules of the exercise require that you *not* rebut the statement maker. You cannot say, "Yes . . . but. . . ." Words such as *however, nevertheless, consequently,* are not allowed. Rebuttals are not allowed. John must listen during the statement of Jane because in Step two "Understanding," he will be required to repeat back the statement.

The most important rule of RDS is that you do not leave Step two until the statement maker agrees that he or she feels understood. If after John gives "understanding," Jane does not feel understood, John must try again. John may ask Jane to repeat the statement or expand on it. John must struggle to repeat the statement in a manner that will lead Jane to agree that she feels understood.

Step Three is *"Agreement." John must agree with Jane.* He must give as much agreement as possible. And he must be honest. If John cannot honestly agree with any part of the statement, he must give minimal agreement. Minimal agreement is, "Jane, I agree that you feel . . ." and John must then repeat her statement. Disagreements must be kept to yourself.

RDS is a sequential discussion in which listening is forced and rebuttals are forbidden. It also revolves. After John has successfully completed Steps Two and Three, he becomes the statement maker and Jane must then give "understanding" and "agreement."

There is no better way to improve communications with your family members than RDS, but communication alone will not save your family. It takes faith to save a family. Faith is turning inward with commitment. Commitment is trusting someone enough to become deeply involved with them. The hard core of faith is involvement.

The eleventh chapter of Hebrews in the New Testament is a description of this kind of faith. It's a magnificent chapter in which the author parades the patriarchs of the past and points out their deep involvement with life.

The author shows us a dimension of depth to faith. It's a degree of depth that we must have if we would find substance in our families. We cannot project ourselves to find assurance of the future of our families, but we can descend into life at its deepest and find the foundation upon which even the future must rest. And so it was with the patriarchs.

The first hero of faith was Abel. Abel brought a lamb to the altar, and his brother Cain brought some grain from the field.

The Scripture says that Abel offered a more excellent sacrifice. Do you know why? If you've ever lived on a farm, you can understand. A shepherd is more deeply involved with his sheep than a gardener is with his plants. Abel nursed his sheep through hunger and cold, through sickness and peril. When he came to the altar, he brought a little lamb, his finest to be sure, and perhaps a pet. Abel was deeply involved in that which he gave to God. So we find his name first in this cavalcade of the faithful.

When Enoch was carried to heaven, the next man of faith was Noah. What was Noah's involvement? He was willing to risk everything in one wild gamble. He built a fallout shelter against the wrath of God, with the deep conviction that God would see him through.

After Noah died, the next hero was Abraham. Here we see most vividly that faith is a family affair. Faith seldom involves individuals. It sweeps up the entire family. Abraham's great involvement was this: God had a plan to raise up a new people. Would Abraham get involved?

No one wanted children more than he did, but there's a lot involved in having children, especially when you're old. Sarah had no desire to kill the family tree with the blight of her barrenness, but she was too old to start a family. Then too this new plan meant leaving the suburbs of civilization for a new frontier in the west. Many people would like to change jobs or communities, but there's too much involved—so they don't.

Abraham did. He left Ur of Chaldeans, moved to Canaan land and started a family. Abraham named his baby Isaac and soon learned that there is more involved in raising a boy than in having a baby. Do you remember that mountain scene where Abraham is preparing to sacrifice Isaac on the altar of God? As children we were spellbound by the story and felt so sorry for poor Abraham. But the scene is not quite as unique as you make it. Many fathers have felt like Abraham. Many fathers have stood at the altar of God, not with a son to be slain but with a daughter to be given away. Here is the great involvement of family life. We raise our children to lose them, and lose them we must.

When Abraham and Isaac died, the next hero of faith was Jacob. For all his cheating and lying, Jacob qualifies to answer this role call of the faithful. Jacob's great involvement was two-fold: (1) When he left home, he did not leave his God; and (2) he fell in love. Do you remember how he met Rachel at the well and worked seven years to have her for his own? The Scripture says the seven years seemed only as a few days, for he was so deeply in love with her. Here is involvement! This is why romance is so eternally popular. It's the one degree of involvement which nearly everyone achieves. It is better to love and lose, than never to love at all—because love can show you what involvement is.

When Jacob died, the next hero was Moses. The Bible says that it was by faith that Moses refused to be called the son of Pharaoh's daughter. Instead, he became involved with a minority group of peasant people. Moses was a happily married rancher with no political aspirations. Why get involved with this peasant revolution back in Egypt? But he did, and by so doing, he answered the roll call of faith.

When Moses died, the next hero was *not* Joshua. Strange as it seems, a prostitute named Rahab is listed. What was her involvement? Of all the people in Jericho, she only feared the Lord. She bargained with the Israelite spies to save her life, but her great involvement was that she insisted the spies grant protection to her family too.

A prostitute can have only two possible relationships with her family. She is either a complete outcast or a total provider. Her family either despises her or depends on her. Dostoevski made us all hang our heads in shame with his narrative of Sonia in that penetrating novel *Crime and Punishment*. Here is a degree of involvement—a depth of faith which few folk attain.

We don't know that Rahab supported her family, but if she didn't, she was despised by them. And to be concerned about those who despise you is a deep degree of involvement. Here ends this roll call of the faithful, not with a pious priest but with a wayward prostitute.

The author of Hebrews did not pick people with no liabilities in the ledger of their lives. The Bible tells us about Noah getting drunk, and Jacob cheating his brother, and the plain bold fact that Rahab was a prostitute. This Hebrew hall of fame is not a collection of do-gooders. These folk stumbled in and out of the same sins which snare you and me. What makes these people, this chapter, so eternal? One quality! These people were willing to get wrapped up with life at its deepest. They had no fear of getting involved in anything, for they had a deep conviction that God was in charge of everything.

If you are to save your family, you must turn inward with a depth of commitment which involves your total person. Faith in the family bond is trust, but it goes beyond trust. It is a posture of commitment. It is a leap of faith. It is like the man who found the perfect pearl. He sells all his property and possessions to purchase the flawless pearl. He sacrifices everything to have the object of a life-long quest.

Faith is flinging oneself into a relationship with total abandon. Faith rules out prenuptial agreements. Faith is total involvement. It closes no door to any room. Jane and John cannot exercise faith in their marriage and qualify their commitment.

The postures of faith and analysis are antithetical. Analysis keeps one on the bank. One shouts instructions to one's family in the rapids. Faith is different. When there is a faith commitment, one flings oneself off the bank into the rapids. John immerses himself in the rapids of life with Jane and vice versa. There are no exceptions. Faith is the posture of a fling.

Faith implies risk. The patriarchs in Hebrews, chapter eleven, were people who took risks. People who wait for the perfect marriage partner are unwilling to take risks. Faith means that Jane marries John with full knowledge that John is less than perfect.

But faith is not foolishness. For Jane to marry an abusive alcoholic is not faith, it is foolishness. There is a painful pattern in which adult children of alcoholics marry alcoholics. This is not faith, because faith is free. To exercise faith one must exercise free choice. The adult child of an alcoholic who marries an alcoholic is not exercising free choice. He or she is repeating painful patterns of the past. They are puppets and they know only one Bible verse: The sins of the fathers are visited upon the children to the third and fourth generation (*see* Exod. 20:5).

We don't become free until we hear the Word of God in Ezekiel 18, "Let it no more be said in Israel; 'the fathers have eaten sour grapes and the children's teeth are set on edge'" (*see* v. 2). We are free when we realize that "the soul who sins, it shall die." We are free when the mosaic of faith is chipped into the vertical walls of our commitment to each other. We are free when we are no longer compelled to repeat the pain of the past.

The yellow brick road to freedom is the footpath of faith. It is also the road to a happy family life.

Summary

How does one go beyond communication to commitment?

First, you must receive faith. Faith is found at the cross of Jesus Christ. The cross was the ultimate involvement, because when Jesus died, the next of kin was God. When this kind of involvement floods the basement of your being, you will be able to commit yourself to your spouse and family. When God enters your life, he leaves the fingerprint of faith.

Second, you must refuse to worship at the shrine of communication. The baal worship of analytical theory and bombastic communication techniques will erode the walls of faith in the superstructure of your family.

Next, *you must remove the underbrush of irrational anger that clutters the forest of your life.* (Join the human race, and stop playing Jehovah God.)

Finally, you must pattern your life after the patriarchs of the Bible. These were ordinary people who mastered the art of involvement.

3

Faith Is the Act of Reconciliation

Faith means turning inward with commitment to your family. This is easier said than done. It is easy to say, "Darling, I love you!" It is harder to live a life which demonstrates this love because living in a love relationship requires the prerequisite of a faith commitment. Faith is not something you *feel*. Faith is something you *do*.

Faith requires work. The Bible talks about faith being the gift of God, and it is. But when we receive the gift, we are directed by Scripture to do the work of commitment. Commitment requires that we work at reconciliation. Faith will not accept estrangement. John may be estranged from God, and he may be estranged from Jane. Faith will not tolerate either of these estrangements because faith comes from our heavenly Father.

The Father of our Lord Jesus Christ is the center and source of involvement. The Father God created the cosmos through an act of involvement. The Spirit of God brooded upon the primeval waters, and the chaos became cosmos through this involvement. When God enters your life, chaos and estrangement leave.

When you receive the gift of faith, your life takes on a new posture. It is the posture of commitment and commitment is hungry. It hungers for reconciliation.

There are two sources of involvement in this world. They are creation and the cross—the creation of our world and the cross of Jesus Christ. When you receive faith, you relive sacramentally the cross of Christ. Here is ultimate involvement. Here the process of creation focused sharp and clear, once and for all, in the person of Jesus Christ. It is at the foot of this cross that we learn commitment. It is here that we become thirsty for reconciliation. It is here that we become doers of the Word. The hardest place to do the Word is at home.

It is better to step toward reconciliation than to talk about it. Moving across the room and sitting next to your spouse is far better than talking about it. And when your relationship is strained, this kind of movement is critical. You can say, "I'm sorry," in a hundred ways without using words. Sometimes difficult words come easier after physical movement has taken place.

There is no reconciliation more difficult than that of a parent and a child, especially when geographical distance is involved. Listen to one of the greatest stories ever told.

Dan Hunt

Dan Hunt was the owner of a country store in Kent County, Delaware. Both he and his store were institutions. Hunt had dropped out of school in the tenth grade, but he was a student of human relationships until the day he died. There was not a marriage counselor in Wilmington who was a more effective therapist than Dan Hunt. He studied what goes on between people like a stockbroker studies the marketplace—ceaselessly. His store was an excuse for him to be at the center of the community. He advertised everything and stocked nothing.

"Dan, you've got the worst darn store on the Chesapeake Bay," Uncle Frank told him one afternoon.

"Frank, how many days have you missed coming to this store in the last thirty years?" Hunt wanted to know.

Uncle Frank rubbed his two-day stubble of beard, "Well, I was sick in bed with the flu in thirty-nine. Likely didn't make it that day," he said, as he smiled his real communication to Hunt.

Hunt would never have called himself a retail merchant; he was a caretaker of people's problems, and he knew it. But Hunt had experienced his own share of problems. His wife had died when the boys were four and six years of age. And for some reason he had never remarried. His brother said it was because he was married to the store. This may or may not have been true, but no one could fault Dan Hunt on the way he raised his boys. He never let his work take priority over the kids. He would have been the first to admit that he had made some mistakes. It's hard to be both father and mother to a pair of youngsters who need more attention than a dozen parents can give. Some people said that Hunt was partial to his baby boy, but everyone knew that he loved them both, would do anything for them. They were all he had.

Hunt was a religious man, and he went to church regularly. He loved the Bible, and at night he told his boys the heroic stories of Samson and Samuel, David and Jonathan, Shadrach and Meshach and Abednego. He tried to plant within his boys a love for life and a reverence for God.

As the boys grew up, they began to develop different personalities. Nick, the older boy, began to put down roots. He could find no meaning in life apart from familiar fields and friendly faces. Dan had ninety acres of land that he let Nick farm. The boy loved the land and would spend hours on Sunday afternoon walking the fields. He said it was to check the fences. The fences seldom needed repairing, but Nick checked them every Sunday afternoon. He needed very little excuse to walk the fields and to enjoy the land. More often than not, Nick would help tend the store after supper. He was everything a father could ask of a son.

Tim, the baby boy, was something else. He knew every traveling salesman by name and would entice them into talking about Wilmington and Baltimore and D.C. And if they could talk about Philadelphia, he would sit and listen for hours. Tim had been out of Kent County only twice in his whole life. Nick had never been out of the county, and said he never intended to. "I was born here, and I'll die here."

"Not me," replied Tim, "first chance I get, I'm going to do me a piece of traveling." To Tim the routine of home life was as dull as the romance of travel was delightful. He went to sleep at night dreaming about the women in Wilmington. "I'd be willing to get drafted just to get out of here," he said.

Two weeks after Tim finished high school, a new salesman from Baltimore stopped by the store. Dan was reluctant to take on a new line of merchandise, but Tim was gullible for a new line of baloney. The salesman enjoyed the rapt attention of the young man, so he embellished his stories of Baltimore women and big-town nightlife. Late that evening Tim and his dad had a long talk.

"There's no reason for me to stay here. Nick has the farm, and you have the store. Besides, I'm raring to roam."

"Son, everything I have is yours. I need you in the store, but if you want your own piece of land, I'll get it for you."

"It's not that, Dad. I just want to get out of here and do my own thing."

Dan had always given his boys a lot of room in which to live. Nick wanted very little, and Tim never had enough. The old man wondered how they could be so different.

"Tim, I hate to see you go. Things just won't be the same around here without you."

"I know, Dad, but I'm bored and want to see a little of the world. I may be drafted next year anyway. I want to live a little before the Green Machine gets me."

"When do you want to leave?"

"In the morning."

"Morning," his father exploded. "Son, I was thinking about the first of the month. In the morning," Hunt shook his head in disbelief. He was faced with the grief experience of all parents, letting their children go. He wanted to keep Tim a couple of weeks in hopes that the young man might change his mind.

"How much money do you need?"

"A couple of thousand."

"Son, that's a lot of money."

"The land you were going to buy me would have cost more," Tim pointed out.

The father was puzzled. "Why do you need two thousand dollars if you're not going to buy land?"

"I want to take a welding course in Baltimore," Tim said. "The tuition is eight hundred and I'll need money to live on while I'm in school."

Hunt had the money, but he hated to invest it in a project that would take Tim away. He looked at the floor for a long time. Finally he said, "I'll write the check." It was the hardest thing he ever did.

Tim left at sunrise the next morning. Dan Hunt was an emotional man, and sometimes he cried. But he had not felt this bad since his wife died. He watched the dust billowing after Tim's car and felt tears wetting his cheeks. He bent double, buried his face between his fingers and shook with grief.

"You did the best you could to raise him right," Nick said to his father in a vain stab at consolation.

"He'll do all right," the father said after his crying had subsided.

"I hope so, Dad."

Tim drove nonstop until he reached Baltimore. He was drunk with the excitement of the city. By the time he reached the outskirts of Baltimore Highlands, a fierce flow of adrenaline was pumping through his system. He could live as loosely as he liked and be as bad as he wished, and he was going to make the most of it.

Tim found a room at the YMCA, and it was the last Christian association he had. The first night he got drunk out of his mind. When he sobered up the next day, he said to himself, "I really ought to look up that welding school, but I want to enjoy the big city first." It was the last time he thought about welding.

He had promised to write home once a week, but he couldn't tell anybody back home what he was really doing. He could make up a story, but that was too much trouble. When the fifth week passed and no word came, Dan Hunt was in agony. He knew that he shouldn't have let him go, but more than that he knew that Tim was hurting. He had an uneasy feeling that his baby boy was in quicksand. Dan Hunt did not sleep for five consecutive nights. He later learned this was when Tim started heroin.

A prostitute had told Tim that the high from skag was better than sex. He couldn't believe it, but no one had told him how much fun sex was. "If you don't like it, you can always stop," she said. Tim didn't like it, and he didn't stop. After the first shot, he vomited until nothing came up, and it was green. "It's always like that at first," she said, "your body has to get used to it." A week later Tim's body not only liked it, it craved it.

Ten days later he was broke. He had blown two thousand dollars in six weeks. Tim got a job sweeping out a warehouse, but his withdrawal was just severe enough to get him fired. He was sweating slightly and having mild cramps when he sat down. The night guard was suspicious, pulled up his shirt sleeve and saw the tracks. "Damned junkie." The next day Tim was fired. He had no money, no job, and was withdrawing from heroin. "How on earth did I get myself in a mess like this?" he puzzled.

That afternoon he sat on a park bench, and for the first time since he saw Baltimore he slowed down long enough to reflect on what he was doing with his life. He had traded his car for a three-day supply of heroin. He couldn't hold the simplest job. He was hungry and didn't have the price of a hamburger. He hadn't paid his rent in six weeks. For a few moments he was intently silent. Something stirred deep within him. Why, he could go home! He knew that he had no right to go home, but something told him that he could. He had paused long enough to let the persistent prayers of his father break into his conscious mind. He could go home!

Tim Hunt hitchhiked all the way to Kent County, Delaware. His father was ringing up a sale when he walked in the store. Somebody said, "There's Tim!" His father looked up and ran and hugged his boy. They all cried for a long time, even Uncle Frank.

When the tears finally stopped, Tim said, "Daddy, I blew it, every penny. But if you'll let me, I'll earn it all back." And the old man cried even harder but through the tears, he said something about "no way."

Then he started shouting like people at a Holiness Revival meeting, "Tim's home, oh, praise God, Tim's home!" It took the old man a half-hour to calm down. In the commotion someone knocked a can of beans off the counter. They were bending over to pick it up when Hunt said, "Stop, leave it there. Frank, I want you to get on the phone and I want you to tell everybody in Kent County that Dan Hunt is giving away groceries." By sundown the joyous father had given away to a rejoicing community every item in his store. Most folks never ate what he gave them. Years later they would say, "See that can of beans. Dan Hunt gave that to me the day Tim came home."

Tim Hunt performed an act of reconciliation. His father responded with warmth and acceptance. No words can capture the symphonic drama of this kind of reconciliation. Tim and his dad went beyond communication. You can too. You can resurrect a loving relationship with the significant people in your life. (The plot of this story was stolen from a man who spent his adult life drifting around his country with an itinerant band of fishermen to whom he told stories about The Kingdom.)

Reconciliation requires that you do something. Geography must be overcome. (Tim hitchhiked home.) Spacial separation must be conquered. It is better to hold hands on the couch than to talk tenderly on opposite sides of the room. Movement toward people takes more courage than talking to people. There is no substitute for physical movement in the reconciliation of relationships.

Reconciliation also involves doing penance. What the Roman Catholic Church has practiced for years is a vital part of reconciliation and communication. We must "do penance" to restore relationships. Words without deeds are cheap. Deeds give words meaning in human relationships.

Deeds also give symbols meaning. Symbols are the mortar that hold the bricks of a family together. Core symbols are the foundation upon which it is built. The evening meal, going to church on Sunday morning, the homestead, the family vacation, and many other traditions may be core symbols in a family. But symbols require deeds of reconciliation. When you sabotage your family, you must "do penance" to put it back together again.

Bringing something home as a gift is only one way to "do penance." You must discover in your own family the deeds which have healing power. Once you have found them, don't lose them. They are precious.

The act of reconciliation is turning inward with goodwill to the important others in your life. Tim could have taken a "pity trip" to some inner sanctum of his soul and brooded forever about his bad luck in Baltimore. He didn't do this. He walked to the curb and stuck out his thumb. He hitchhiked home. He performed an act of reconciliation. You can too.

Sometimes it is necessary to be reconciled with your parents before you can make things right with your children. Many people get divorces when their real fight is with their parents. People try to get from their spouses what they failed to get from their parents. This is doomed to failure. Your spouse can never give you the kind of nurturing you failed to get from your mom and dad. If you expect it, you will be angry with your spouse and not know why. If you're disappointed with your spouse, and don't know why, it's probably because you're expecting the impossible. Don't divorce your spouse. Reconcile with your parents, even if you have to hitchhike home.

For almost twenty years, I have earned my living as a family therapist. I've seen a hundred couples divorce when their marriage could have been saved if they had exercised the courage to seek reconciliation with their parents. How is this done? First, you must get in touch with your anger toward your parents. Then you must work through this anger, until you can forgive your parents. You know that you have forgiven them when you can sincerely say, "Given the circumstances, they probably did the best they could."

This kind of reconciliation is a painful journey. It requires just one thing to do it—faith. Faith means that we accept our world as imperfect.

I once had a tomcat named "Buttons." He was a mongrel feline who refused to admit his backalley ancestry—a black cat who turned prematurely gray. He was also temperamental, stubborn and self-centered.

But for all his shortcomings, the cat was remarkably perceptive. When one of the girls was sick, Buttons intuitively knew it and would sleep on her bed until she got well. But when I got sick, Buttons couldn't care less. (And there were times when I could have used a few feline strokes!) If I had let myself, I could have gotten depressed over the matter. It's not that Buttons bit the hand that fed him; he just ignored it. I could have told myself that this was awful, terrible, and disgraceful. At times I did.

The hard, cold reality is that there was nothing awful about Buttons' behavior. It was unpleasant, but it wasn't terrible. There is no law in Georgia which says tomcats must love their masters. Sometimes I think there should be, but in my more rational moments I know what my problem was with Buttons. We both thought we were head of the same household. This power play persisted until poor Buttons died. And that's not terrible; it's just the way it was. Ours is not a perfect world, and it isn't reasonable to expect tomcat tears to fall on our rejections.

Once my daughter Donna was trying to describe a cat's paw. She wound up with the phrase "death in a fur coat." It is like this with life. Beneath the warm fur of life are the hard claws of death. This isn't terrible; it's just the way it is. Tomcats kill birds. "Bite their little heads off. Nibble on their tiny toes." And that's just the way it is.

Nevertheless, we expect perfection in our world. We don't like cars to cut in front of us, traffic lights to turn red, parking places to be full. These are minor irritations, but I'm concerned about a more serious matter.

We often expect perfection in ourselves and in the people who relate to us. We expect our children to love us without ceasing. We want them to be fair, honest, and faithful. If they aren't, we are quick to brand their behavior as *terrible*.

Listen to the story of an angry woman. Susan Blalack entered the office with anger tattooed on her face. She was mad. She was mad at John. She was mad at me. She was mad at men. A hundred nonverbal words exposed the hatred that she stockpiled in the basement of her being.

She was a short, thin woman, and I wondered how so much hostility could be packed in such a delicate and graceful body. Susan was thirty-seven but could have passed for twenty-seven, had it not been for the anger that tightened the muscles in her face. I was determined to relax those muscles.

Susan and John had come to me for family therapy. I began to work at once.

"I would like to hear you discuss your problem, but I want you to do it in a way that may seem a little awkward at first. I want you to sit back-to-back and take turns talking to each other," I said. Resistance! Immediately! Susan glued the posterior of her anatomy to the chair. A blow torch could not have moved her out of it.

John Blalack was less reluctant to follow my suggestions. He had forgotten Susan's birthday and had gone on a trip with his mother. He expected me to give him a professional spanking.

John quickly perceived that I was not in the spanking business. "John, would you help me turn these chairs around, so the two of you can sit back-to-back?" I said. He did. He was a long, lean six-foot-two, thirty-eight-year-old banker. John was "on good behavior" and was trying hard to please me.

Susan wasn't. "Susan, I would like it if you would sit here," I said in my most professional tone (which sounds a little like God with a sore throat). Susan shot a laser beam of hostility into my brown eyes which could have melted a pantheon of therapists.

Finally, I took Susan's wrist, and with a gentle tug I pulled her into the chair. "Susan, I want you to collect your thoughts, and I want you to share them with John," I said.

They were now sitting back-to-back in the middle of my office. "Susan, what would you like to say to John?"

"I don't want to tell that 'bleep' anything."

"John, I am very angry at you," I interpreted her statement.

"Yeah, John, what you did wasn't right, and you know it." With that, Susan was off and running with a catalog of grievances. She spit them out like a faulty toaster propelling burnt bread across the kitchen. I was able to paraphrase some of her statements and give them a feeling content.

Later in the counseling session, Susan was glaring at me—long nonverbal streaks of red. "Susan, you're mad at me," I said.

"No, I'm not mad at you," and then she paused. "Well, maybe I am. I want John to suffer as much as I have, and you're not helping."

"I'm not helping what?" I puzzled.

"You're not making him suffer."

"Susan, what do you want me to do?"

She broke down and cried. She cried for several minutes, and some of her anger came out. But the basement of her soul was cluttered with big crates of irrational hostility. Some of this anger I couldn't get up the stairs at this session, but in the course of therapy the two of us cleaned out that basement. Susan had been angry at her own mother for years. She was the first-born and had felt abandoned when her little brother was born. When she worked through this anger, the firetrap deep inside her was removed, and she could think clearly for the first time since her marriage went sour.

How did Susan do it? First, she cleaned out her basement. Anger breeds anger, and the center of your being will become a rat's nest of bitterness if it's not cleaned out.

But ventilation of negative feelings alone will not put your internal house in order. You must surgically remove your anger, if it has no reality in it. Susan asked over and over, "How could he do this to me?" There followed a litany of woe and weeping. "It's terrible, disgusting, awful, disgraceful."

In reality, the behavior of her husband was unpleasant and a source of embarrassment. It was painful, but it wasn't terrible. I refused to let her describe her position as Armageddon. It wasn't the end of the world. If your marriage is sick, you are better off if you repeat this remnant of reality about six times a day. Susan did.

I did something with Susan which most counselors don't. I talked about suffering. I talked about the Bible. I talked about the ministry of pain. Susan was a religious woman and together we read Romans 5:3-5.

> . . . we rejoice in our sufferings, knowing that suffering produces endurance, and endurance produces character, and character produces hope, and hope does not disappoint us because God's love has been poured into our hearts. . . .

Susan knew the first part of this piece on pain. She knew about suffering. She had a bad relationship with her father, a worse relationship with her mother. She knew all about pain and suffering. But she knew only one way to talk about it. Her way was the Jehovah Complex. When she saw pain, she said, "How could this happen to me?" Unconsciously, she was saying, "I am Jehovah, and God isn't supposed to suffer."

When her husband forgot her birthday, she said, "How could he do this to me?" Susan wasn't pleased when I pointed out she was playing God, that she was pretending to be Jehovah, but slowly she began to crawl down from her high pedestal and begin a journey to her family of origin. It was a long painful trip, but it ended with forgiveness.

"Susan, we live in our imperfect world where pain and suffering are permanent fixtures," I said six months into the therapy. It took some time, but finally she came to face this. Like Susan, we too are forced to face the valley of the shadow, the hills of hurt and pain. None of us is Jehovah. We were born in pain. We will live in pain. We will die in pain. None of us is above it. None of us is God, and the radical news of the New Testament is that God suffers too.

The important thing is not the presence of suffering. It is how we look at it. Paul said, "I rejoice in it . . ." (see Col. 1:24). Perhaps he didn't know the kind of pain we struggle with—arthritis, lupus, kidney stones, broken marriages, and lost jobs. Maybe, he didn't know all that. He did. The Bible is a catalogue of the pains of Paul. No one knew more suffering than he did—physical, mental, and emotional. Paul had been through a form of hell. But how could he rejoice in it? Paul knew a secret. He knew the fruits of suffering. He knew about endurance and character and hope. He had tasted each of these, and they all tasted good.

Paul also knew the bitter fruits of pain. He knew that some people become hostile and vindictive, hopeless and depressed. Paul had read the book of bitterness, but he refused to interpret his suffering this way.

Paul had a second secret which colored his picture of

pain. He knew God's Spirit, and he believed that through the Spirit of God, faith would be poured into our hearts.

Love was all that Susan really wanted. She desperately wanted to be loved. She falsely assumed that if her husband forgot her, he really didn't love her. She was wrong. She later learned just how lovable she was. She also learned that she was partially to blame for what was wrong in her marriage. She learned what her mistakes were and how to avoid them in the future.

In our last session together, I said, "Susan you have one more bit of homework to do."

"What's that?" she wanted to know.

"Forgiveness."

"Forgiveness? I've forgiven my mom. I really have."

"Yes, you need to forgive John, too."

"I'm not sure I can do that," she said.

"Why not?" I asked.

"Well, because you just can't forgive forgetfulness. It is like adultery."

It was then that we read together that incomparable eighth chapter of the Gospel of John:

> and Jesus went to the Mount of Olives.
>
> At daybreak he appeared in the Temple again; and as all the people came to him, he sat down and began to teach them.
>
> The scribes and Pharisees brought a woman along who had been caught committing adultery; and making her stand there in full view of everybody, they said to Jesus, "Master, this woman was caught in the very act of committing adultery, and Moses has ordered us in the Law to condemn women like this to death by stoning. What have you to say?" They asked him this as a test, looking for something to use against him. But Jesus bent down and started writing on the ground with his finger. As they persisted with their

question, he looked up and said, "If there is one of you who has not sinned, let him be the first to throw a stone at her." Then he bent down and wrote on the ground again. When they heard this they went away one by one, beginning with the eldest, until Jesus was left alone with the woman, who remained standing there. He looked up and said, "Woman, where are they? Has no one condemned you?" "No one, sir" she replied. "Neither do I condemn you," said Jesus, "go away, and don't sin any more" (vv. 2-11).

By the time we reached verse eleven, Susan was crying. She was crying hard. But when she stopped, she took a deep breath and she was born again. New life began to enter her body.

Reconciliation requires forgiveness. Reconciliation also requires that you and your family have a communal commitment involving a mission outside of yourself. We'll talk about this in chapter 7 "The Community of Hope Is the Church."

4

Focus on Your Needs

Some people say, 'I need him, therefore I love him,' but it's not that way with me," the coed said to her college roommate. "With me it's the other way around. I love him, therefore I need him." Her roommate quickly agreed, putting love before need fulfillment seemed to be the natural order to both of them. Love was primary in relationships, and it was important to keep your priorities straight, they thought.

In the small town where I grew up, the farming women would have taken issue. "Honey, you've just been seeing too many movies," they would have rebutted. I agree with the farm folk. The romanticism of the latter half of this century is a mental attitude that we have been taught by magazines, movies, and television.

It is a delicious state of mind, but unfortunately romanticism will not sustain a marriage relationship. Romantic love is thrilling, exciting, but it won't last. The farm folk

71

would describe romantic love the same way they described sweet food at breakfast, "It won't lay by you." It is not romanticism that will save your family, but rather it is turning inward to the fulfillment of your own needs.

You must focus on three of your needs: *power, privacy,* and *security.* These are by no means all of your needs, but my clinical experience in marriage and family counseling points toward family failure for those people who don't meet these needs. They are the Big Three of family survival. Don't neglect yourself.

There is an old saying: "The most important thing a man can do for his children is to love their mother." This is true. But to love someone doesn't mean that you neglect your own needs. Parents cannot love their children if they neglect their own needs. Parenting requires that you fulfill three marital needs.

Power

Power in a marital relationship revolves around who makes the decisions, who makes the rules, who structures the framework of the relationship. Sometimes women delude themselves into thinking they don't want power. "I don't want to make decisions; I just want to be a good wife and mother." Some religious groups teach women to be "passive Pauline wives." It doesn't work. No one wants to lose all the time. You don't need *all* of the power in your marriage relationship, but you need some of it.

If you want to save your marriage, you must use your portion of the power. How do you do it?

1. *Often the spectator spouse must get a job.* If you are unemployed in our society, you may be relegated to a powerless posture. Women with small children must find a source of child care. The ideal situation is for Dad to share

the child care. If this isn't possible, a day-care center must be found. If you can't work full-time, get a part-time job. If you earn only a few dollars a week, it is your money. It symbolizes that you are not totally dependent on your spouse. It is money you can spend without asking permission. Do it. "It is so degrading to have to always ask for money," wives say to me. Of course it is! In American society you are valued for what you can earn. Money is power and you need your share of it.

2. If you are a passive spouse, *you must assert yourself in the decision-making process.* "I'd like to talk about it" is a six-word sentence you must learn to say. Repeat it to yourself six times a day. Then when your spouse slips into a decision-making stance, spit it out.

"Hey, how would you like to go to the beach this weekend?" When a dominant spouse says these words, it is not a question, it is a decision. He or she expects a passive response:

"Neat-oh!"

"Oh, wow!"

"Sure, honey, whatever you say."

Don't give it. Give back those six words of power. "I'd like to talk about it." Your spouse will be upset. Expect it. Accept it. "I just said that I'd like to talk about it. I don't have as much input into decisions around here as I would like. I just want to talk about the trip." If you do this, your relationship will get worse before it gets better. But you can get your part of the power. You'll have to grasp it; no one will hand it to you— not your spouse, not your pastor, not your marriage counselor. Only *you* can get your part of the power.

Power in a marriage has to do with which spouse is the participant and which is the spectator. The spectator spouse is the one without power and usually is the one without a job. He or she sits on the sidelines while the participant spouse reaps the glory, makes the money, and monopolizes the decision-making process. When the spectator spouse gets bored sitting on the sidelines, he or she will sabotage the participant spouse. This may end the marriage. It usually destroys the balance that makes the relationship work. It is an excursion into undiluted pain. Everyone loses. Everyone hurts.

A much better alternative is for the spectator spouse to become a participant. There is no law which says that both spouses cannot be participants. Actually the game of parenting is played much better with two people on the court. How do you change your role? First, *find out what is important in your community* (something with market value). Second, *do it;* if not full-time, part-time. Third, *give yourself permission to be number one.* Risk success and when it comes, relish it. You've earned it.

As mothers need more economic power, fathers need more nurturing power. Dad needs to spend more time with the kids. He needs to get more involved in the day-to-day decisions affecting the children. One of the best ways to do this is for Mom to take a trip alone and let Dad care for the kids.

Privacy: *A Case Study*

Some people need more privacy than others, but everyone must have their own space in which to recharge the batteries of their psychic selves. Romanticism teaches that you need only intimacy. Don't believe it. People need both privacy *and* intimacy, and they aren't prepared for the latter until they have met their need for the former. Unfortunately, many spouses interpret their need for privacy as a lack of love. "Why don't you want me with you? We used to be together all the time." And the disenchanted spouse is remembering an earlier period, perhaps courtship, when the intoxication of the relationship was intense. But you don't recall the "spaces" in your relationship. Romanticism trains us to remember only the intimate moments. Intimacy is too intense to be sustained indefinitely. You need maintenance periods of privacy in which to be by yourself all alone.

Matthew Sink was a medical technologist who took biology twice before he made a *B* in it. He was twenty-four, thin of stature and thick of head. Matt was bright, but he wasn't very smart. His IQ was above average, but his interpersonal relations were awkward and forced. Matt was a tagalong little brother who never grew out of it. He wanted a symphony of relationships from his marriage, but his repertoire of possible interactions was exceedingly narrow. His emotional appetite was enormous, but his ability to satisfy it was limited. At times he became discouraged and failed to apply the brain power that he had.

No one was more acutely aware of this than Matt himself. "I know I'm socially limited, but I'll find a woman who'll make up for it," he said about himself in college. Matt looked for her incessantly. He'd fantasize marriage with every female who entered the library. Sometimes this made it difficult to concentrate on the genetics of the plant kingdom. If a coed sat down at his table, biology had absolutely no appeal.

Matt was a toucher and often regretted not having become a physical therapist. In a movie he would look for a woman to sit by. Then he would slowly and cautiously try to touch her in some way. Although he seldom made contact, he always tried. *This is just dumb,* he would say to himself while inching his foot closer to the woman sitting next to him. He knew the odds against finding a woman who wanted to touch a total stranger in a darkened theater were astronomical, but he sat through many a dull movie making futile attempts. He often wondered why he had such an insatiable thirst for physical contact. Maybe his mother never held him when he was a baby.

"There's a recurring abnormality on your X ray," the doctor said to Matt the summer before his med tech internship. The doctor's tone was as flat as his face was expressionless. Matt thought he heard him saying, "You've been condemned to die the third week in August, and you'll have to go now because I'm very busy." The doctor's monotone continued. "There's a series of tests which we will have to run. It'll be more convenient if you're hospitalized." Matt heard him saying, "Your confinement begins immediately." Immortality was one of Matt's basic assumptions. He began to question it, when the hospital began the conditioning process called "admittance." It was an exercise in dependency. Good patients depend on their doctors—totally. To reach this conditioned-reflex state, Matt was deprived of his clothing and natural habitat. He was very carefully trained to respond to a controlled stimulus.

"You can see it yourself," the doctor said as he pointed to the quarter-size spot on the chest X ray. "It's either a tumor or TB. It's not high enough to be TB, so it's got to be a tumor."

Matt thought he heard him saying, "You'll die, if you don't do exactly what I tell you."

"Let's check you over," the doctor said, as he started a thorough physical exam. Matt much preferred TB to a tumor. His deepest fears were confirmed when the doctor looked directly in his mouth without wearing a mask. It had to be a tumor.

"I can tell you now that we'll have to operate," the doctor said.

Three weeks later they did. The tumor turned out to be a swollen lymph node that was diagnosed as sarcoidosis, a condition about as dangerous as a bad cold. But a staph infection occurred in the wound. Matt's fever shot up to 104 degrees. He was transferred to another ward and placed in a private room. For two days he was watched closely by an especially qualified nurse. The first day Matt didn't know she was there. When the fever began to fall, he realized that he was being attended by the most touchable human being on the planet Earth.

June Sylvester was a divorcee with a six-year-old daughter. She was a shy, sensuous kind of woman, reserved and seductive. There was an inner depth about her that added to her mystique. Her teeth were crooked, but in some strange way, her imperfections only made her more alluring. When Matt first saw her, he thought he had found fantasyland. "Are you for real?" he said. June didn't know whether he was flirting or getting better. She soon knew it was both.

"You're worth a thoracotomy and a staph infection," he told her on the afternoon of the second day.

"The way you've improved, you won't need me tomorrow," she teased and told the truth at the same time. Matt made her promise to stop by and see him the next day. June enjoyed his flattery so she did. She even helped with his physical therapy, which involved considerable exercising of his left arm and shoulder. This meant that she was touching Matt. Although the exercises were painful, Matt was intoxicated by her touch. Every time her hip brushed his arm, he desperately wanted to reach out and pull her to him.

They were married three months after Matt left the hospital and two weeks before he began his medical technology internship. It was not the best of times to get married. Between Matt's studies and June's shift work schedule, they didn't spend a lot of time together.

They told themselves that everything would be different when Matt finished school. It was. It got much worse. Matt was aware of this downward spiral, but he told himself that

June would never leave him now that he had finished school. "If she stood by me through all of that, she'll stand by me through anything. Besides, our sex life is good," Matt said to himself. Both of them relished touching each other, at least in bed. Matt was aware that June didn't touch him as much as he wanted when they were out of bed, but he was convinced that she would never leave him. He would never let her go. "When you've got a good thing, you hold on tight and don't let go," Matt told his brother.

Matt was a good father to June's daughter. He made a habit of reminding June of this. "Every girl needs a father, sometimes even more than a boy does," he would say. June didn't talk much. As their marriage worsened, she talked less and less. Matt passed it off as just the way she was.

One fall afternoon, Matt came home early. He found a note on the chest of drawers:

MATT, JENNY AND I HAVE LEFT. YOU ARE A VERY FINE PERSON,
BUT I DON'T WANT YOU IN MY LIFE ANYMORE. JUNE.

The next day at work, he was served the divorce papers. Matt met June on the hospital grounds the following afternoon.

"Matt, I just don't want to talk about it. My mind is made up."

"I knew you were unhappy, but you wouldn't tell me why. How can you just walk out on me like this? June, I need you desperately."

June sat down on a bench. "You're not going to like this, but I've got to tell you. You've followed me around like a puppy dog for three years. I can't go from one room to another without you behind me. You've suffocated me, and I can't take it anymore."

Matt had never heard June speak four consecutive sentences. He didn't know she had it in her.

"June, I'll do anything you want me to."

"I just want you to leave me alone. I want to be able to go out at night without having to explain to you or anybody else where I'm going."

"June, you can go out as much as you want."

She would not yield. "Matt, you don't understand. You and I are finished. I don't want to live with you anymore."

"But I need you so much. What'll I do?"

"That's your problem."

"What about Jenny? She needs a father."

"She managed very well before I met you, and she'll manage without you."

Matt followed her to the car. He was still begging when she shifted into reverse and backed out. He pinioned his hands in the open car window and walked backwards with it. "You're going to be lonely."

"Privacy with loneliness is better than invasion with boredom," June said.

"Why?"

"There is hope."

"You can't do this to me," he pleaded.

June turned left and drove suddenly and completely out of his life.

A recurring theme in the marriage myth of America is that your spouse should guarantee that you will never be lonely again. This leads to a leaning posture in which spouses suffocate each other and make privacy difficult if not impossible to obtain.

Privacy, like power, will not be handed to you. You must assert yourself to get it. Many Americans commute to work in the solitude of their own car because it is the one of the few sources of privacy that they have. It is the most expensive manner known to modern people to get privacy.

You may feel embarrassed to even ask for privacy. Don't. Try being honest, "John, I just need to be by myself for a little while. I've had people coming out of my ears all day, and I need to be alone for a few minutes." John may not like it. He may fume and say that you don't love him anymore. If he does, assure him that you love him more than ever, and that as soon as you get back from your walk, you would like to be with him. Then go straight to the door—don't look back—and have yourself a nice long walk, all alone. You've earned it.

If June had said this, she could possibly have saved her marriage. Matt needed less privacy than she did. As a med tech, he had more privacy than June had as a nurse. He could have learned to give June more space at home in which to recharge her batteries.

You also need privacy with your children. Many parents are never emotionally close with their kids because in the hectic hurry of parenting they neglect to meet their needs for privacy. This is particularly true for single parents.

Security: *A Case Study*

Marriage is many things in the Western world: a sacrament, a socially acceptable relationship between adults, a rite of passage, a holy union, but it is most of all a source of emotional security. It is the principal center of stability in our human relationships. Its great importance as an institution today points up the need that we have for stability and structure in our lives. We don't like to be lonely—*ever*. So we carefully structure our lives to avoid the chaotic swings of human emotions and the instability that can result.

No one wants to grow old all alone. We pick partners for life in hopes that death will not destroy our principal plan for companionship. And if it does, we marry again, or we structure our relationships with children and friends to fight off the shadows of solitude. We want and need emotional security.

There was a time when women depended on marriage for economic security. To some degree, this is still true. There is, however, an increasing movement of the female gender toward other institutions for financial security, not the least of which is the marketplace where women compete on their own merits. Marriage is and will remain the choice of most people for emotional security. For all its faults, the institution of marriage can protect you from the "screaming lonelies" on Friday night—but the marriage bond is not perfect. There are no guarantees against the silent sounds of empty days and long lonely nights. Elizabeth Edwards learned this the hard way.

There were no poor people in the little town of Balboa on the Pacific side of the Canal Zone. There weren't any rich people either. But there were many lonely people, especially among those who lived in separate houses. The town was owned by the Panama Canal Company. Most of its dwellings were apartment buildings with four families to each unit, but section chiefs and division heads lived in separate dwellings.

Balboa was a peculiar blend of the bucolic and the tropical. It was Williamsburg, Virginia, translated into the tropics, the seat of the Canal Zone government tucked into the hills that crowd down on Panama Bay.

Elizabeth Edwards inherited both the beauty and the loneliness of Balboa. In Panama the trees bloom. They are giant bouquets of red and purple and yellow. The little town was brilliantly beautiful. So was Elizabeth. Her dark silky hair was seductively tropical, her flawless complexion as pure as a virgin beach in the Perlas archipelago. She had a grade-school beauty that matured with each year.

But her father was a division head. They lived in a separate house, and her loneliness was brutally intense. She
grew up in an affluent isolation which is the birthright of
only children raised in a colonial setting. Her parents could
afford a live-in maid, but they couldn't afford to pay for
friends like rich people can. Elizabeth's father was a work-
addicted engineer. Her mother was a compulsive socialite.
Both lifestyles are desperate escapes from loneliness. Both
offer temporary solace to adults, but they leave children marooned in jungles of solitude.

Elizabeth was raised by a Panamanian maid. Olga was
doting and protective, but she refused to find friends for the
little girl who worshiped her. When she was in grade school,
Elizabeth would walk to the Balboa Post Office every day, not
to get mail, because no one ever wrote her. She hoped the
postal clerk would speak to her. "Well, hello, Elizabeth!" he
would beam and she would explode with excitement. Some
days he was busy, and she would wait unnoticed for a half-
hour before she gave up and returned home. On those days
she wished for crooked teeth. On her way home, she walked
past the orthodontist's office. It would be fun she thought to
have someone touch her once a week. But her teeth were
perfect, and many weeks no one—not even Olga—would
touch her.

When she was twelve, Elizabeth would cross the street in
front of her house without looking. She hoped that she
would be hit by a car. Then, when she went to Gorgas Hospital, she would find out if anyone cared enough to come to see
her. Olga would be there and her parents would make a big
scene, but some days she doubted if anyone else would come
to the hospital. When she was really depressed, she would
stop by McGinnis Chapel at the Balboa Union Church.
Sometimes in the secret solitude of that remote little chapel,
she would feel better.

When Elizabeth was in Balboa High School, many boys were hesitant to ask her for a date. "No girl that pretty would ever go out with me," they said. Many less attractive girls were more popular than she. Elizabeth was a senior before a date had the courage to park with her on the causeway at Fort Amador. They were watching the green starboard light of a ship in the channel when Elizabeth suddenly realized that Dwayne was more interested in her body than he was in nighttime traffic in the canal. She tried to camouflage her excitement, but her hard heavy breathing gave her away.

Elizabeth's emotions darted back and forth between desire and fear. Her heart was like the train that transits the tropical jungle of the Isthmus every hour only to return at once to the Pacific side. It knifes through deep foliage and the mystic moods of the rain forest. It runs restlessly in perpetual motion between the Atlantic and Pacific sides of Panama. It was like this with Elizabeth. She wanted sex but she didn't want it. Her mind raced back and forth between passion and terror, and there was a jungle of tangled emotions inbetween. But, if letting Dwayne do what he wanted with her body was the price of companionship, so be it. Dwayne was excited with his exploration of her body. Sex, however, was not Elizabeth's deep thirst. Please God, she didn't want to be lonely ever again. Eventually, the long-dormant sex drives of the young couple led to a togetherness which Elizabeth both relished and assumed would last forever.

After their first year at Canal Zone College, Dwayne and Elizabeth were married at the Balboa Union Church. Dwayne got a job in the dredging division, and they moved into an apartment in the little town of Gamboa. Everything was perfect. They made bookcases out of whiskey boxes and displayed their bottle collection in rustic splendor. They would spend hours hunting for bargains in Panama City. A modern painting or an old cabinet that they both liked was a major "find." They would put it in a special place and call in their neighbors to *oh* and *ah* with them.

Interior decorating didn't last forever. The third year of their marriage, their living room was as crowded as their lives were empty. Dwayne was restless. He joined a little theater group which performed out on the causeway at Amador where they had first courted. They both auditioned for parts, but Elizabeth could not project herself into a role. She never got a part. At first, she busied herself with stage management and lighting. While Dwayne improved in his acting, Elizabeth lost interest in staging. By Dwayne's third play, Elizabeth was staying at home. There was an empty and hollow feeling that inched its way back into her bones. Dwayne stayed later and later for practice. When he stumbled up the stairs at midnight, he was emotionally drained. He wanted a drink and bed.

Elizabeth had crying spells. There was no other way she could get Dwayne's attention. "I feel like I'm losing you, and I don't like the feeling."

"Elizabeth, I've got needs that are being met in acting. I don't want to give it up."

"It's lonely here at night."

"Find something to do."

There were many things which Elizabeth could do; the problem was to find someone to do them with.

It was in March of '72, during the dry season, that she and Dwayne and another couple sailed their twenty-six-foot sloop to Contadora in the Perlas Islands. It was one of their rare good times together. They had left the Balboa Yacht Club about midnight, and with a strong breeze off their port beam, arrived in the Perlas Islands at sunrise. They had set a heading of 120 degrees on their compass and, although the compass light had burned out, Elizabeth relished the excitement of holding a flashlight on the pedestal. Dwayne took the wheel with one hand and encircled Elizabeth's slender waist with the other. Elizabeth was enraptured.

They anchored on the leeward side of Contadora Island and spent the day swimming and shell hunting. Dwayne did not normally sail through the island chain at night, but there was a full moon that night. Everyone was a little high from the drinks they had concocted after supper.

"Why not?" someone said.

"You only live once."

"I've never seen a more beautiful night in Panama Bay. Would be a shame to waste it sleeping."

They set sail at dusk and three hours later, after two more rounds of drinks, were approaching the island of San Jose. Dwayne was leaning against the stern pulpit, when a wave hit the boat from the starboard side. Normally, he would have caught the backstay and kept his footing. His reflexes were slowed by the booze. He lost his balance and was overboard!

"Dwayne fell over!" Elizabeth screamed.

"Where's the flashlight?"

Someone found it and pointed into the dark abyss off the stern of the boat.

"We've got to find him with the light," Elizabeth shouted as she turned into the wind and tried to start the auxiliary engine.

"There he is!" someone shouted as the beam of light crossed a distant wave.

"Oh, please, God, keep the light on him," Elizabeth begged.

And then the light turned orange. It lasted a moment longer, and all was black. Elizabeth was hysterical. Their guests did not know how to handle the boat. By the time Elizabeth pulled herself together, valuable time had been lost. They motored back and forth all night, but they could not find Dwayne. Their flashlight batteries had burned out the previous evening. Someone radioed a distress message to Contadora, and by dawn a rescue boat had reached San Jose from Balboa.

They found Dwayne the next day sitting on the beach in a cove where legend had it that a German pig farmer had been murdered. The tide had washed him ashore and although semiconscious, he had crawled up the beach to a piece of driftwood. He collapsed upon it and awoke the next morning clinging to it in desperation. When he realized that he was safe, he did some serious thinking.

He first resolved never to drink again. Second, he promised himself to have a long talk with Elizabeth.

She was on the bow of the boat when it turned into the cove where he was sitting. They screamed simultaneously. Elizabeth jumped overboard, swam to the shore and embraced her husband. They both cried for a long time.

"Dwayne, it's all my fault," Elizabeth sobbed. "I don't deserve to have you back." She was crying hysterically. Dwayne held her tight and some of the trauma worked its way out.

"Hush, hush. Everything's going to be all right," he said as her convulsions began to ease.

Their friends had blown up their inflatable raft and were rowing over to meet them. Dwayne had some difficulty getting into the unstable raft, but Elizabeth pushed while their friends pulled. Dwayne was back on board.

"Sweetheart, I did a lot of thinking back there on the beach," Dwayne said on the seven-hour sail back to the mainland. "I promised myself that whatever the problem is between us, I would do my best to work it out."

It was an hour before Elizabeth stopped crying. When she did, she told Dwayne about her long history of loneliness and confessed that she had expected too much from him. As the boat heeled to starboard and the tropic breeze blew them home, she promised not to lean on him ever again.

Elizabeth kept her promise. She made new friends, started a new hobby, and joined a book club. And then a strange thing happened: the emotional security that she had failed to find when she sat home and pined for her husband came to her when she looked for it outside her home. And it came to her from Dwayne. When she stopped leaning on him, she became a much more desirable partner, and he made the initiative to spend more time with her.

There is just no way that one person can meet all of your emotional needs. If you lay this impossible burden on any one person, you are going to alienate that person. Your primary relationship with your spouse will improve if you cultivate secondary relationships with other people.

The best way to find security in your marriage is to turn inward with faith. Turning inward in desperation as Elizabeth did lowers one to the posture of begging. Nothing will destroy your chances for emotional security in your marriage more quickly. Don't beg. Don't pursue your spouse. Pursuing emotional security is like pursuing a butterfly barehanded. Don't do it. Turning inward with faith means that you don't lean on your spouse; it means commitment without intrusion.

In any romantic relationship the partner who pursues is in a posture to be manipulated by the partner who flees. It is a precarious position. It also doesn't work. It is turning inward to the bare cupboards of empty loneliness.

Try something different. Turn inward with faith. Commit yourself to your spouse, but don't intrude and don't interrogate. This kind of focus will make you a much more interesting person to your spouse. You'll become a participant in life, and that alone will make you more fun to be with.

The same principle applies with your children. When spouses fail to find emotional security in each other, they often turn to their children. Parents need to be committed to their children, but if parents try to live vicariously through their children, if won't be a faith experience. It will be intrusion. It will be enmeshment. It will not be a freeing experience. It will be entrapment.

Parents often become fused with their children. Fusion is living your life reacting to the emotions of another person. If this person is your child, the family will be enmeshed. Your happiness will depend on the happiness of your child. When he or she is up, you'll be up. When he or she is down, you will be down. This is not a faith experience, because faith is free. There is no freedom in fusion; none for you or your child.

When you turn inward with a faith commitment to your child, it is a freeing experience. Faith is a better way to turn inward because it has a partner called "hope." Hope will lead to a broader network of possibilities than exists in the inward domain of dyadic exclusiveness. There is no hope with fusion.

5

Faith Looks Deep Within

Step Four of the Alcoholics Anonymous twelve-step program stresses the importance of a "searching and fearless moral inventory" of oneself. Biblical guidance for parenting has the same requirement. A moral inventory must deal with values. Values are not created by individuals. They are handed down from generation to generation.

The decalogue says, ". . . I the LORD your God am a jealous God, visiting the iniquity of the fathers upon the children to the third and fourth generations (Exod. 20:5). A prevailing theme of the Old Testament is the overriding influence of previous generations upon our everyday behavior. (See Psalm 109:9, Isaiah 14:21, 65:7, Jeremiah 32:17, 18, Lamentations 5:7.) Since the principal source of our guidance in parenting comes from the modeling we see in our families of origin, it behooves us also to make a "searching and fearless moral inventory" of our past and present.

Buried deep within our bones are at least three or four

generations—perhaps the entire human experience—but the past three or four generations directly affect our daily process of living. The mistakes of our ancestors are reincarnated in the parenting of our children. Every day in the practice of therapy, I see Jane and John making the same errors with their children that their parents made with them. It doesn't take much research to learn that their grandparents made the same mistakes with their parents. Jane complains about her critical mother and criticizes her children in the same sentence.

A principal theory of family therapists is that unfinished business in one generation is passed down to the next generation. Family therapists are trained to see what is going on between the generations and how this unfinished business is contaminating John and Jane's parenting of their own children. The tool most used to understand the intergenerational is the genogram.

A genogram is a family tree of three or four generations, but it goes beyond most genealogical charts in that it shows brothers and sisters as well as parents and children. Systems theory is used to interpret the genogram in that family therapists believe the whole is more than the sum of the parts. The whole must include how the parts interact. With a genogram the therapist wants to teach his or her clients how the generations interact.

I do not believe anyone has made a searching and fearless moral inventory of his or her life until he/she has looked honestly at the past three or four generations bearing down upon the present. I also believe parenting is impossible until one understands and grapples with his or her own intergenerational past. I have wrestled with my intergenerational issues for years and know through my own pilgrimage that past issues have played a decisive part in my parenting mistakes. Faith looks deep within. Biblical faith remembers the

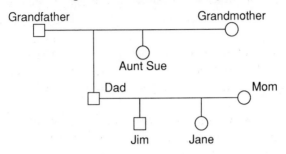

Figure 1 **The Jones Family**

past. Nostalgia remembers, but it is careful to select only those parts of the past which will not disturb the status quo of the present. Family photo albums picture only part of the past. Biblical faith as exercised by the pre-exilic prophets remembered the past "warts and all." (*See* Amos, Micah, Isaiah 1, Hosea.) It is this kind of searching and fearless moral inventory which parents must make. Those who are justified by faith will live (*see* Hab. 2:4). Life as a parent requires the inward scrutiny of faith. It is only when we are committed to the Father of our Lord Jesus Christ that we can be honest in our parenting.

Case Study 1

This case study will focus on how unfinished business between a father and his own father affected the father's parenting of his son. The genogram in figure 1 shows three generations. The case study will attempt to show what was going on between the generations.

Jim was a ten-year-old lad in trouble with his father in the mid-1940s for what was called "playing marbles for keeps." This was a childhood game in which boys would draw a circle on the ground and place an equal number of marbles within the circle. They would take turns "shooting" from the perimeter of the circle. All of the marbles which a boy was able to knock out of the circle, he was entitled to keep.

Jim's Dad was opposed to the game and forbade his son to play it. The problem arose in that this game was the principal social activity of Jim's peers. Jim didn't want to be left out.

There were two taboos in the Jones Family. One was sex. Jim and Jane had been carefully trained not to ask questions about sex. No one ever said to them, "Don't ask questions about sex," but they knew not to do it. It was like smoking in church. There weren't any No Smoking signs posted, but everyone knew not to do it.

The other taboo in Jim's family was Grandfather Jones. No one ever said, "Don't inquire about your paternal grandfather," but Jim and Jane knew not to do it. Jim had never heard any reference to him at all. He was like a black hole in the solar system of the Jones Family. Grandfather was the elephant in the living room which *no one* dared to mention.

Jim was in college before he summoned up the courage to say, "Somebody tell me something about Grandfather Jones." He learned a little from his father and a little from his father's younger sister, Aunt Sue.

The story he was able to piece together went like this: Grandfather Jones was a gambler. He earned his living playing poker. Grandmother Jones was a very proud woman and was mortally wounded by this unacceptable career choice. Grandfather had been a bricklayer when she married him.

Grandfather was playing poker on one occasion with the county judge. As usual, Grandfather was winning. The judge accused him of cheating, "Jones, you're winning because you're playing with a marked deck."

"You're right, Judge. We're playing with a marked deck," Grandfather said as he looked down at his hand. "But, Judge, in your old age, your memory is slipping. This is a marked deck, but it is *your* deck. You brought the cards tonight."

Grandfather had figured out the judge's markings and was beating him with his own deck. The judge was embarrassed and never forgot the night. Nor did he ever forgive Grandfather.

A few months later Grandfather had a run of bad luck and wrote a bad check to cover a gambling loss. The man who received the check took Grandfather to court. Unfortunately, the case was tried by the judge Grandfather had embarrassed. The judge sent him to prison for eight years.

This was more than Grandmother Jones could take. "I never want his name mentioned. Never again!" And it wasn't—until Jim went to college.

The unfinished business between Jim's father and Grandfather Jones was that Jim's father had never forgiven the old man for being a gambler and going to prison. Once Jim's father had framed "playing marbles" with the unfinished business of his past, that is, gambling, there was no way he could have a rational discussion with his son about it.

"Well, I just don't see what's so bad about playing marbles," Jim exploded.

"It's gambling; that's what's wrong."

"Why is it gambling? You have to be a good shooter to knock the marbles out. Luck has nothing to do with it."

"Don't dispute my word. It is gambling, and it will ruin your life."

Jim never understood any of this. His father was able to convince the elementary school principal of the evil of marbles. If boys were caught playing marbles at school, all the marbles on the ground were confiscated. Jim wondered what happened to all those thousands of marbles. One day while sitting in the principal's office for another offense, he stuck his head in a large walk-in closet adjacent to the side door of the office. There on shelves, from the floor to the ceiling, were hundreds of quart cans of grapefruit juice. On closer inspection, Jim learned that they didn't contain juice at all. They were all full of confiscated marbles!

Most parenting problems come from the intergenerational. We want to give our children autonomy to make decisions that will serve their enlightened self-interest, but we can't *give* freedom unless we *have* freedom. The only way we will ever have freedom is to work through our anger at our parents and then forgive them.

Case Study 2

This case study is about anniversaries. We celebrate wedding anniversaries but we observe many other kinds. The most powerful of anniversaries is the one which deals with death. The Abernathy family never realized the power of this anniversary in their lives (see figure 2).

The Abernathy Family was an institution peopled with beautiful human beings. At least Jason thought so. There was not a more attractive couple in Marlborough, Massachusetts, in his opinion. Dad was a perfect example of masculinity—classic features chiseled from the gods of antiquity. Mom was incredibly beautiful. She dressed immaculately. Jason was proud of his parents. He never really understood why his mother left his father and went back to Saint Paul. It happened on his fifteenth birthday, the beginning of his ninth year of school.

Figure 2   The Abernathy Family

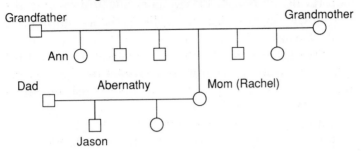

Mom was the fourth of six children reared in a devout Lutheran family. When Mom was fifteen, her father died, and her life fell to pieces. She had been his favorite. Unlike most parents, he boldly admitted his favoritism.

"That's not fair, Rachel gets anything she wants," Ann, the first-born, said.

"*Mein kind,* I am the parent. You are the child. Parents outrank children. I will favor Rachel whenever I want to." When the old man spoke, it was with the finality of a Prussian soldier. He commanded everything in life except death.

After her father died, Rachel was forced to quit school and go to work. Only her younger brother and sister got to finish high school. Mom was always embarrassed to have to tell people that she dropped out of school in the ninth grade. But quitting school was not as hard as enduring the wrath of her brothers and sisters. They turned on her with a vengeance. They didn't care that she was beautiful. They bled her of every liquid ounce of love her dad had intravenously fed her.

"Why did he do this to me? How could he leave me like this?" Rachel asked over and over as she struggled through dark days of abandonment. No one ever answered her question. Rachel never asked it out loud, but it raced in circles around the center of her mind like a restless squirrel in a revolving cage.

Rachel got married to escape the sibling torture of her family. She wanted her husband to spoil her the way her father had. When he didn't, she pouted. "Well, my father would never treat me like this."

"I'm not your father," Dad would answer.

"No, you aren't. You aren't half the man he was." The marriage was never truly functional, but there was no real danger of dissolution until Jason entered the ninth grade. The delicate balance which Mom and Dad had maintained through sixteen years of marriage was thrown off by some unseen force that dictated their parting.

In no way did Mom want to leave Jason and his little sister, but she packed a suitcase for herself alone, called a taxi, and left for the train station. She never again returned to Massachusetts.

When Jason turned fifteen, it became an anniversary for Mom. She was fifteen when her Dad died. The only way she knew to celebrate this anniversary was to leave someone. Her husband had not met all of her needs. Why not leave him? Jason looked like her father. Why not leave Jason? This separation and subsequent divorce caused the pain Mom needed to inflict, but it in no way served her enlightened self-interest.

She had failed to forgive her father for dying. This created enormous pressure for her to leave her first-born when he turned fifteen. Mom had failed to say *good-bye* to her father. This made it difficult to say *hello* to other men in her life. It made it especially hard to say *hello* to her fifteen-year-old son. The decalogue said, "The sins of the fathers are visited upon the children to the third and fourth generation."

When Jason gets married and has children, the odds are that his marriage will end when either his first-born boy or his second-born daughter is in the ninth grade. Anniversaries are that way. They gain power with each successive generation.

Part 2

Parenting
with Hope

6

Turn Outward to Save Inward

Without hope, faith turns into romanticism, the assumption that two people and their offspring can meet all of each other's emotional needs. Hope in the New Testament is apocalyptic; it looks outward to the end of the age. As a boy I learned what this means. I learned to look out from the poverty in which I grew up, out from the drudgery of picking cotton ten hours a day, out from the pain and embarrassment of not meeting bills.

"On Jordan's stormy banks I stand and cast a wishful eye." I sang with hope—hope that the Lord would return soon. I looked outside Tipton County, outside the Mississippi River bottom. I looked to heaven. People who have never known poverty call it "pie in the sky, bye and bye." It was more than that. It was hope. Only people who suffer know what hope is.

Parents suffer for many reasons. One reason is that they have been taught only to look inward. The Bible says that

looking inward alone is a mortal sin. Ananias and Sapphira
(Acts 5) had faith, at least in their dyadic exclusivity, but they
didn't have hope. (And they underestimated the God who
judges hearts.) As a marriage and family therapist, I work
with people every day who are dying in their heart, mind,
and soul because they have not hope. They don't know how
to look outward to the church and the Lord himself.

Jane Eckstein

Hear the story of a modern Mary Magdalene and how she
learned to look outward. She sat there and she cried. "My
husband doesn't want me anymore." Her body shook from
the explosion of sadness within her. "He said he never loved
me; he just put up with me—and now he can't even do that."

Jane Eckstein was a bone-thin, twenty-three-year-old
single parent. She had two children, no job, and no market-
able skills. She was totally depressed. The birds were singing
in the tree outside my window. She didn't hear them. It was
spring, and the flowers were blooming. She didn't see them.
Her world view was the dark brown of the muddy river in
which she was drowning. Jane Eckstein was ninety-five
pounds of depressed humanity.

She was without hope. The most important thing in her
life—her marriage—had just died. Her life was falling to
pieces. I spent an hour a week with her for several months.
We struggled with two recurring questions. Is there any real
hope in a world riddled with divorce and depression? How
can you parent two children when you are emotionally bankrupt?

What do you do when you've built all your hopes on one
person and that person leaves? Mary Magdalene must have
asked this question. She was from a small fishing village on

the Sea of Galilee—a town called Magdala. She had left her family and friends to follow Jesus. The Bible says that seven demons had been cast out of her. This meant Jesus had healed her of a severe emotional problem. And she had followed him. She lived in that small band of poor people who wandered the hills and valleys of Galilee with Jesus. There was no church building in those days—no one place where one could go to fellowship with the faithful. The only way to learn about Jesus was to join the itinerant band of poor people who roamed the rivers and roads of Palestine.

Mary did. She was grateful for her health and determined to spend her remaining years in the shadow of the man who had made her whole. Never had anyone accepted her the way Jesus did. Mary was not the only woman who followed Jesus. There were many, and Mary loved the fellowship of her vagabond sisters. For three short years she was more alive than she had ever been.

Then it happened. Her world fell apart. The center could not hold. They took him away. The day Jesus died, Mary and her friends stood on a distant hill and watched the crucifixion. Stunned and depressed, they shuddered as the setting sun sent the shadow of a cross down the valley into the creek of their depression.

Would the sun ever rise again? Would they ever know another human relationship—one that was open and honest, real and exciting, secure and satisfying. As the darkness destroyed their view, they knew that death—his death—had ended their pilgrimage of hope.

Mary would go back to Magdala and die. A dozen people had said she shouldn't leave. A dozen more said she would soon return. Now she would. But she could not leave without that most ancient solace all grieving people, the decent burial of the beloved dead.

This all happened on Friday. Mary came back on Sunday

morning. Why she came back, she did not know. She had planned to be halfway to Magdala by now. Jesus was dead, and dead men don't make meaningful relationships. But she could not leave the Lord in life; she could not desert him in death. The sun was not yet up as she groped through the trees, feeling her way through the darkness.

There were swells of grief which washed the shores of her soul; there was an earthquake of pain which shook the basement of her being, and she could not tell if the ground quivered or if her heart quaked. When she reached the tomb, the entrance was open, and the body was gone. It was then that God's messenger said to Mary and her friend,

"Don't be afraid."

"I know what you are looking for."

"I know that you are lonely and depressed."

"I know that you are without hope."

"But you won't find what you are looking for here."

"He is gone."

"You will find him in Galilee. Go and tell the others."

And they did. A few days later Mary and her friends went home to Galilee, but Mary went home to Magdala a new person. Now she had hope. The angel had given her something no one could take away—not the governor, not the soldiers, no one! Now she had hope, a deep-seated confidence and conviction which death itself could not destroy. But it was more than confidence, it was a new life posture. She had learned to look outward. Jesus would come back. Until that day she would have the church, an outward and visible sign of an inward and spiritual hope experience.

I hadn't seen Jane Eckstein for a year. I had often wondered how she was doing and if she survived those difficult days of divorce and readjustment. She was so thin. The last time I had seen her, I knew she had hope. She said she was going to make it. Her depression was relieved; her anger had been ventilated; her decision making was improved, but none of this will put food on the table. She couldn't type, she couldn't sell, she hadn't finished high school, but she had hope—a thin unadorned ray of pure hope. And that was all she had.

It had been a year when the intercom buzzed and the secretary said there was a woman to see me. I told the secretary I had a full load and couldn't work in another client. The secretary said that Jane Eckstein was in the chapel and that it would take only a moment.

She walked in with hope in her eyes. She was still a thin, hesitant young woman, but she had lived with hope for a year, and it made a difference. She had gone to a school for welfare mothers and had gotten a job. She was thrilled at being able to make it by herself, and she had stopped by to tell me about it.

"Jane, I'm glad to see you—you look so good," I said. "I knew you could make it, but, wow, you are doing better than I ever dreamed."

"It was faith and hope," she said, "since my divorce I have been even closer to my church. I really dreaded going back to Sequine. I was the first person in my family to get a divorce. I felt like I had this dark-brown spot on my dress that wouldn't wash out. I hated going back to church and wearing that dress. But I did, and they accepted me, and I love them for it. I'm closer to my girls than I have ever been. I'm not a perfect parent by any means, but I know six families at church who love my girls and will do anything for them."

This all happened twenty years ago, and I have not seen her since that day—but I am sure Jane Eckstein has hope.

The Christian faith doesn't promise a rose garden; it promises a crucifixion. There will be Gethsemanes and Golgothas, but through Calvary we will find hope. There will be separations and sickness; there will be pain and parting—but there will be hope. We never fully experience hope until death and resurrection are played out in our own experience. We must die to the narcissistic individualism of our culture, and we must be reborn into the community of the concerned.

Nowhere is this more important than in the institution of the family.

There are only two possible relationships between husbands and wives—love or war. Both are ancient, both are intense, but love is better than war. Love is that constant maturing relationship between a man and a woman that recreates itself through the very process of releasing itself. Love is security. It is that bedrock certainty that one person in this world will share the pleasure of your company tonight. Love is caring. It is caring enough to get involved in the life of another person. It is the total immersion of yourself into the liquid center of your life partner. It is that mystic mingling of two human beings into a harmonious blend of their psychic selves.

Love is sex and the explosion of it. It is one of the main events in the arena of marital relationships. It is the high-wire focus of fun in the center ring of an ongoing relationship—but love alone is not enough. I have counseled a hundred couples who had a good sex relationship and nevertheless suffered a bad marriage. Good sex is supposed to make good marriages, but a mountain of clinical evidence says "not necessarily." You must have faith and hope—and they must come first.

The question is *how*. How do you stop fighting and start loving at your house? How do you translate a hostile relationship into a loving one? How can you change your own attitude from that of a critical spectator to that of a loving participant? How can you find hope?

For two years I conducted a monthly marriage workshop in San Antonio, Texas. I was new in the marriage business at that time and was uncertain how to structure the four hours that I had with a dozen couples each month. I had inherited a program that included lectures by clergy people, doctors, and financial advisors. It was "the dead burying the dead." It was not that the lectures weren't well presented; they were. But it was a group of external authority figures talking down to a group of people about how to live their most intimate relationship—their marriage. It didn't work.

I had recently completed a twelve-month internship in Los Angeles in marriage counseling, which included endless hours of group therapy. I was full of confidence and ideas. I let all the lecturers go and decided to structure a group setting in which the couples would sit in a circle and share with each other. It didn't work. Subgrouping is the kiss of death to the group process. Each month I had a dozen subgroups, and I lacked the experience to mold a dozen dyads into a functional whole. I marshaled all my powers of confrontation. I "stung" both individuals and the group for their lack of responsiveness. It didn't work. Each couple raised the ramparts higher. They withdrew into their coupleness.

Someone suggested dividing the groups by sex. The men would relate better with only their male peers in the room; likewise with the women. Dividing the sexes would also break up the couples. They would then become more open, especially on matters of sex. They didn't. They weren't open on anything.

Then I tried the hope principle. I brought in a young couple who had worked out many of their problems and was willing to share the experience with the group. This worked. The group opened up. The couples became responsive and learning took place. Month after month the couples sat around a big table, and I marveled at the power of people to help each other. It was a setting in which the engaged couples learned to look outside of themselves. They knew they had relationship problems. When the presenting couple created an atmosphere of hope, they began to think, *Well, maybe there is some hope for us too.* It was anticipation of better things to come. But it was more than that. It was learning to look outward to a group process in a Christian setting. All healing in human relationships comes from the Holy Spirit and the Spirit usually works where "two or three" are gathered in his name. We must learn to look outward.

Tony and Linda

Linda was lonely, feeling left out. She hoped Mr. Malone would be in his office. She wanted to talk to someone she could trust. The sign read PASTOR'S STUDY. She knocked on the door and cracked it open.

"Hello, Linda." Mr. Malone said as he extended his hand. "Come in. I'm really pleased you came."

He looked confident and clerical. Linda wondered if he would be shocked at what she was going to tell him. She and Tony had decided not to live together any more. They had been active in Grace Church, and Mr. Malone had agreed to talk with her.

"I really need to talk about Tony," Linda said as she looked her minister dead in the eye.

"Sure," the clergyman said in his lowest, most pastoral tone. "This must be a great shock to you."

"It really is." Linda looked at the floor. "I never thought my marriage would end up this way. I could not believe it for a long time."

Linda didn't know why she needed to talk about Tony, but she did. Even more, she wanted to talk about what went wrong in their relationship. She knew she should have talked to a marriage counselor years ago, but that was water over the dam.

"I know it's hard for you to talk, but it might help," the fifty-year-old man said. "Why don't you start by telling me what kind of person Tony is. I don't know him as well as you do."

Linda took a deep breath, called up some long-dormant courage. "Tony is the kind of person who can sell you a wagon load of hay and have you believe that every piece of it came from the manger of Jesus."

Mr. Malone looked startled.

"I know it seems crude to be so blunt, but I've got a lot I want to say. I'd rather be direct."

"That's quite all right."

"His physical presence is overwhelming. He played left guard at Ole Miss and was captain of the team," Linda paused. "As you see, Mr. Malone, I'm just the opposite. I don't weigh a hundred pounds and I've never been captain of anything. I'm twenty-five, but I feel like forty-five."

"You feel really bad," the minister reflected.

"Yeah, I really do."

"Could you tell me about some of your problems?" Malone wanted to know. "What did Tony complain about before he left?"

"Tony didn't have any problems apart from me. His super aggressive lifestyle met his needs. I was the problem."

Malone looked at his left hand, then at Linda. She was not a classic beauty but she was pretty in her own manner. Her facial beauty was not overwhelming, but she was attractive in a suburban sort of way. She was delicate, and each tiny bone looked thirsty for tender, gentle strokes.

"In college Tony wanted sex in a slam, bam, thank you ma'am manner. There was no way that I could enjoy it in the backseat of a seventy-two Plymouth with nearly three hundred pounds of left guard suffocating me. It was like being run over by an angry rhinoceros who was in a hurry," Linda paused, wondered what the clergyman was thinking.

"We had sex but it wasn't good—at least not for me." She felt like she was confessing a cheating scandal to her high-school principal, but she had asserted a part of herself, and she was glad of it.

"There was a lot of status in dating the captain of the football team. My friends swooned every time they saw him. You know, I was really somebody."

The minister nodded as if he knew what she meant.

"Our public life was so exciting I tried to forget our private problems. I told myself that in time Tony would learn to be tender. I said it over and over like a commercial. I was hoping the repetition would create the love I needed. It didn't." Linda was visibly sad.

"After graduation we got married and Tony went into the life insurance business. He sold a million dollars worth his first year, and two years later he was sales manager. We never had money problems but sex was something else." Linda looked at Malone. He was tall and lean, more attractive than she was comfortable with. Maybe she could tell him everything. He was more accepting than she thought he would be.

Malone said that he wanted to see if he was hearing what she was saying. While he echoed back what she had just told him, Linda's mind roamed over the feverish years gone by.

After three years of marriage, she was aching for tenderness. She had faked orgasm for two years, and Tony demanded a performance twice a week. She had tried to discuss her needs, but Tony was always too tired or too busy.

Mr. Malone had finished his paraphrase. "Am I hearing what you're sáying?" he wanted to know. Linda didn't care whether he heard or not; she just wanted to talk and not be put down for her past.

"Yes, that's right," she said politely. "Things got so bad last January that I left Tony. I went to Wilmington and stayed with my mother," she sighed, took a deep breath, and continued. "After two long months, Tony called and wanted to know when I was coming home. I asked him when he was coming after me. He hung up and drove straight to Wilmington."

"Did things improve when you got back together?" Malone wanted to know."

"Not really. Tony was nice for a couple of days. And we just didn't talk about sex."

"That became taboo."

"Yeah, the subject, but not the practice. We had it more, and it meant less. I needed tenderness and I couldn't find it with Tony. I told myself that Tony would mellow with time, but he didn't."

"What did you do then?"

"I cried a lot. Then I decided what we needed was a baby. If Tony became a father, he would surely change."

"Then you had Jenny."

"I centered my whole life on that little girl."

"Was Tony more responsive to your needs?"

"No. He just became jealous of Jenny."

Linda was crying now. Hopelessness washed out of her self like the repetitive rolling tide. "Finally I realized that I had to talk to someone."

"I'm glad you did. I'm not a marriage counselor, but I have a friend who is. Would it be all right with you if I called and made an appointment?"

Linda said it would. She and Tony saw the counselor for six months and their marriage was saved. The counselor was helpful, but Linda really saved her own marriage. Doctors don't deliver babies; mothers do. It's the same with marriages. Counselors don't save marriages. People do. Linda did.

How did she do it? First, *she refused to believe that communication can cure things.* Her counselor said that if she and Tony learned to talk to each other, everything would be okay. It didn't work. They talked calmly and they fought fiercely. When they turned inward, it didn't work. Things got worse.

"I'm bored" is a direct communication, but Linda's expression of it failed to help her marriage. It only started a big fight. "I'm lonely" just made Tony mad. "I need tenderness" always drew a painful rebuttal from the big guy.

Linda gave up on communication as a panacea *and looked for something they could both do together and enjoy.* It turned out to be a small sailboat. At first this didn't help either. There is something about a boat which turns the calmest man into a raving tyrant. Linda was patient. She was addicted to water and wind and sail. She also wanted to save her marriage. She wanted to make love the main event in her relationship. As Tony became more confident in his seamanship, he became more pleasant in the boat.

Sailing is hard work. There was rigging to maintain, the bottom to scrape, the sails to mend, the sea to master, navigation to learn. Self-reliance became a life and death issue. The work was therapeutic. Their sex life improved. There was a new kind of union between Tony and Linda and Jenny that grew out of their physical labor in maintaining and sailing their boat.

It doesn't have to be a boat. Any activity that taxes your physical and mental capacities and turns you outward will help to save your family. It could be gardening, camping, backpacking, biking, hang gliding, swimming, jogging— whatever. What you must do to save your family is turn outward with hope.

Once a family finds something they all like, the battle is two-thirds won. If your marriage has deteriorated to the point where you can't say, "Let's buy a boat" and get the message across, then you need to see a marriage counselor. But many people can rediscover love in their life through mutual work alone. Physical exertion is the natural state of the human species, and it is the seed bed for a hopeful relationship. When you turn outward to the physical, the quality of your family life will improve. The Bible says, "Six days shall you labor." Machines have taken away most labor, so we must create artificial labor. Labor is strenuous physical activity that has a survival connotation.

In a marriage-enrichment workshop, a couple was asked to list the three times they felt closest to each other. The wife's most meaningful moment came when the two of them were pulling up crabgrass in their backyard. Mutual work is therapeutic. Don't end a day without it.

The key is mutuality. Most spouses do physical work but not together. John does the yard work while Jane does the housework or vice versa. They seldom do physical activities together. Mutuality also implies survival. The physical activity must be something your family can fantasize to have survival value.

For example, if you all enjoy gardening, you can create the fantasy of surviving on the vegetables you grow. If you enjoy backpacking, you can create the fantasy of "us against the wilderness." "Us against the ocean," is an easy fantasy to manufacture in a sailboat. The fun of survival has been lost in our postfrontier culture. It was vital and real in the eighteenth and nineteenth centuries. Jane and John had no family problems when they were struggling together on the frontier. There were no marriage problems when the Indians were attacking the fort. The principle is this: If you are engaged in physical activity of a survival nature, your family will work. The Bible says, "Six days shall you labor." The family that labors together will live together.

Sailing is hard physical work, and sex was better for Linda after a long sail. Tony was never the most tender of human beings, but the sheer physical labor of sailing and the immense satisfaction of being self-reliant at sea took much of the rhinoceros out of him. Tony needed the hostile environment of the open ocean to show him how much he needed Jenny. She would snuggle in his lap when he sat at the wheel.

After the first step of sailing, Linda took a giant leap in her relationship. She consciously decided *to lean less on Tony and to actively relate in a meaningful manner to other men and women in her church.* You can too. You can broaden your repertoire of adult relationships. Your primary relationship needs to be in a good state of repair before you seek happiness in secondary ones. But once you have done maintenance on your marriage, don't hesitate to develop friendships in the community.

Linda had depended on Tony to meet all of her human and emotional needs. This was impossible. No one human being can meet all of your needs. Even the expectation of it will destroy the possibility of love in your life. Linda learned to relate to men in nonsexual yet intimate ways. When she did, a new avenue in her life opened up—the avenue of hope. She became active in church life at Grace Church. She went on backpacking trips without Tony. She really got to know the neighbors next door; she joined a group of women who taught themselves how to paint. She worked hard at making new friends, at enriching relationships through the myriad pastel shades of her own responsiveness. She turned outward to both the physical and to the social. As a consequence, her inward relationship with Tony improved.

She said, "Hey, I'm an important person all by myself alone." This affirmation in no way denied the importance of her relationship with Tony. It really enriched her marriage and gave it new life. Somewhere deep inside herself, she said, "I am a child of God and that alone is almost enough." When you lean on your spouse, your relationship becomes stagnant, growth is stopped, and your potential as a human being is limited. When you lean on your children, your family becomes enmeshed and autonomy is destroyed. You spend your life reacting to the emotions of other people.

When you choose to become involved with people other than your spouse and your children, you give yourself a new posture in human relationships. It is a posture of hope. If you are involved only with your family, you develop a posture of leaning. It is tragic to live and die on this planet of four billion people and to have known only two other people really well.

People are gregarious by nature. Always have been, always will be. You do one of three things with your gregariousness: *you actualize it, you fantasize it,* or *you suppress it.* Linda decided to actualize her gregariousness. She made friends with new men and women, and she cultivated these friendships.

A second option is fantasy. If you choose fantasy, you wait in your Betty Crocker kitchen for the fairy godmother to bring you Prince Charming. This is "waiting for Santa Claus," and it is a recipe for a three-course experience in pain. If you fantasize your gregariousness, you will become a pathetic hermit.

If you suppress your gregariousness, you will become maliciously competitive or openly hostile. At least a hundred people in the last twenty years have described some competitive activity to me (golf, tennis, bowling, and so forth) and concluded by saying, "It keeps me out of trouble." By this they meant they would have preferred to have turned outward in a social setting, but they considered the matter too risky or too scary. So they structured their time with something competitive and did it as passionately as possible. "It keeps me out of trouble," they said with a resigned low-grade desperation. Actually, their competitive activity kept them *in* trouble.

The fierceness of competitive sports, which many people center their lives on, is an attempt to suppress basic human needs. The need for variety in our relationships is sufficiently strong to make us frustrated when we suppress it. We become irritable, hostile, and physically sick. Tennis won't really keep you out of trouble. It is great exercise but a poor substitute for the richness of human relationships.

Competitive activity works better for the young than it does for the old, but it is a repression of the human thirst for relationships. It is not possible to compete fiercely with your opponent and at the same time to enter a warm relationship with him or her. There is only one way to go: actualize your need for a variety of human relationships. Some people have a greater "people thirst" than others. But everyone has to quench his or her thirst sometime. Don't dream about it. Do it. Join a club; attend a church; take a course in auto mechanics; go back to college. Do it.

The third and most important step Linda took in restoring love to her life was *to learn to value herself.* She had to look outward to do even this. Once, when she was a little girl, her mother caught her admiring herself in the mirror. She never forgot the stinging rebuke she received. "Who would stop a galloping horse to look at *you*?" She was carefully trained not to enjoy herself. She was taught that it was vain to consider oneself attractive. It was sinful to focus on any part of one's body with admiration. She fantasized her mother would die if she even so much as said, "Wow! I've got beautiful arms." She began to turn outward. She looked at her body. She focused on her beautiful arms.

"Enough is enough is enough," Linda exploded. "If you've got it, flaunt it" might have been an overreaction on her part, but this self-assertive statement helped Linda break out of mother's prison of self-inflicted put-downs. She began to focus on her good features. "You know, my arms are beautiful." Then she began to look at her personal qualities. "Hey, I am sensitive to people's feelings. I can respond to people in a variety of ways."

Linda developed a new sense of self-worth that led down streets of gratitude she had never traveled before. When she became grateful for herself, she found a new freedom. She broke out of her self-inflicted confinement, and she began to explore new relationships. She learned to give compliments. "I like your blouse" was a new sentence she found she could say and mean. Linda had to make a complete about-face to focus outward, but she did it. You can too.

In the two possible relationships between family members, love or war, the first can quickly turn into the latter. No one knows why, but no family need stay the way it is. You can save the inward essence of your family, but you must turn outward to do it. Linda entered community and saved her family. Hope is found only in community, but real community is hard to find these days. When Jane and John were defending the frontier fort, community was a given. This is no longer true. Today Jane and John must search for community.

A group of people does not in and of itself constitute community. Something more is required. At least three prerequisites must be met. The people must have:

1. a common historical past
2. a common present struggle
3. a common future hope

Community is always the gift of the Holy Spirit. The Spirit is the wind. He blows where he wants to. We cannot dictate to the Holy Spirit. We must wait upon him. In our waiting, however, we are better off, if we don't quench the Spirit. Scripture indicates that the Spirit will create community only where the above listed prerequisites are met.

I believe the church has the best chance of meeting these prerequisites. It has a common historical past, a shared history of values and traditions that go back at least three thousand years. Therapy groups appear to create community, but no therapy group has a three-thousand-year history. Jane and John need the structure of community that can only be found in the church and its two millennia of history, tradition, and values. When you turn outward, be careful what you turn outward toward.

When the church is the universal Church, when the local congregation becomes one with the body of Christ, the church will be a group of people with a common present struggle. They will have a mission. They will want very much to do something. Mission means more than retiring the debt on the church building. That may, in fact, be a very present struggle, but a sense of mission looks outward, beyond the edifice of the church to a greater calling. Mission is what binds a group of people together in the body of the Lord. Mission is what makes us community. The edifice is almost irrelevant.

When you are looking for a church, look for a group of people who pray, "Come, Lord Jesus, come!" Community requires a common future hope. Sometimes when we get the new church building paid for, we become "at ease in Zion" and we lose our sense of community. The Spirit heals us when we eagerly await his coming. Community happens when we experience the pain of the present and still believe that God owns the future. The curtain on the last scene has not fallen. Community requires that we believe the tragedy of the present will usher in the triumph of the future.

Jane and John can't experience community by themselves. Most of their marriage problems are caused when they try. John cannot meet Jane's need for community and vice versa. The two of them must look outside of their relationship to the church to get their need for community met.

How can you turn outward to save the inner core of your family? Follow this proven path:

1. Work as well as talk with your spouse.
2. Put a sense of survival in the work which you do.
3. Make friends with adults other than your spouse.
4. Actualize your gregariousness.
5. Learn to value yourself.
6. Look at your body and appreciate the beauty of it.
7. Become more involved in the community of faith.

These practical steps don't sound romantic. Hollywood love dramas never focus on this kind of solution; but with these seven principles of hope, you can save your own family.

The principle is this: You must turn outward in hope to save inward. The solution to your family problem will be partially found outside of your family. Often, we find hope when we turn to our friends.

The Friend at Midnight

Jesus tells us in Luke 11:5–13 about this in the parable of the friend at midnight. It is a wonderful story which could have happened to Joseph when Jesus was a boy. The story begins at midnight, that kind of night when in Nazareth only the scavenger dogs are prowling the streets. There is a knock at the door. Luke is the only Gospel writer to record this parable. He was a doctor and knew what it was to hear a solitary knock at midnight.

"Who is it?" Joseph calls from his crude pallet in the one-room house. The voice of a friend answers. "What do you want?" Joseph barks.

"A relative unexpectedly dropped in and I'm out of bread," the embarrassed voice answers.

"Well, I could care less," Joseph growls.

"If you would lend me three loaves of bread," the voice in the dark pleads, "I could feed my guest."

In ancient Palestine, bread was baked once a week. The various families would take turns using the village oven. In some ways their bread baking was similar to our use of a launderette. The troubled host in our parable has a little cheese, a quart of wine, but no bread and baking day is not till Friday. He needs three loaves of bread, one for the guest, one for himself, and one to have left over. He could not put his guest to bed without breaking bread. Common courtesy demanded a midnight snack. Joseph realizes all this, but he is in bed in a one-room house. If he gets up to give his neighbor bread, he will wake the baby. The door is barred, not merely shut and locked. The twist of a key will not open it. A heavy bar must be removed.

"Don't bother me," says Joseph, "I will wake the whole family if I get up." The neighbor insists he must have some bread. Shamelessly he pounds on the door.

"That incessant knocking will wake the baby anyway," Joseph mumbles to himself. He gets up and fetches three loaves. The mist of sleep is still in his eyes when Joseph unbars the door and stuffs the bread into the waiting hands. The man in the dark cannot thank him enough. He goes home feeling warm and good.

Joseph quickly forgets the troublesome night, but his

neighbor never forgets it. When years later the neighbor attends Joseph's funeral, he tells the son (now a young lad) about the night his dad got out of bed to give him some bread. Why is such a humble event so pregnant with meaning and life? This parable has the ring of reality because it tells us to turn outward to friends. Jane and John are certainly friends, but they need to turn outward to other friends.

A friend is somebody to go to. Jesus says, "Which of you shall have a friend and shall go to him at midnight?" (v. 5). Going to one another in times of joy and sorrow is what life is all about.

What joy is there in succeeding, if you don't have a friend with whom you can share your success? This sharing of joy is what made the missionary witness of the early Christian so effective. When Andrew met the master he was overjoyed. He had finally found what he had always sought. He immediately ran to tell his best friend, his brother. To the first-century disciples, Christ was a joy to share with their friends. Much of the New Testament is some disciple's letter to a friend. Both of the books written by Luke are letters to his friend Theophilus. We don't know anything about Theophilus except that he was Luke's friend. But look what we would lack if Luke had not shared the joy of the gospel with his friend. We would not have that eternal second chapter, nor that magnificent fifteenth chapter about a prodigal son returning home, nor that vivid twenty-third chapter about the day our Lord died. Five of Paul's letters were written to his friends. First and Second Timothy were written to a young minister friend; Titus was written to encourage and instruct a young missionary; Philemon was written to give safe passage to Onesimus a runaway slave; Philippians was written to explain the return of Epaphroditus to Philippi. Much of the New Testament would be missing if the early disciples had not been moved by the Spirit of God to share the joy of the gospel with their friends.

A friend is someone to tell your joy to. Actually sharing your joy with a friend is a mark of humility. You are saying, "I'm not big enough to hold this to myself; I want to share it with you." When you turn outward this way, you begin to find meaning in the maze of life.

A friend is someone to share your sorrow with. This also requires humility. You are saying, "I am not big enough to bear this problem by myself, I need your help." Here is a dimension of depth which we need in our daily lives. The troubled host at midnight learned that friends are what God has made for our needs. No wonder he felt good as he walked home. He was beginning to learn to turn outward in times of crisis.

For three thousand years the world has loved the story of David and Jonathan. Here is what friends can mean to one another. Jonathan was the crown prince of Israel. He was the first in line to succeed his father as king. But there was another contender for the throne, a shepherd boy from the hill country whose name was David. David was not actually seeking the throne, but everything he did was kingly. Saul, the king, was insanely jealous of David's military prowess, for he knew that David had won the hearts of the people. Saul knew that if the people had their way David would be the next king. Jonathan knew this too. If Saul should succeed in killing David, then Jonathan would follow his father as king of Israel. But David was Jonathan's friend.

In an immortal scene, David goes to Jonathan to learn if it is safe to return to Jerusalem. Jonathan endangers his life to learn his father's disposition. He returns to the field where David is hiding and tells the lad that the arrows have gone beyond him, which by prearranged signal means for David to flee for his life. But David cannot leave without telling his friend good-bye. He exposes himself to the danger of the open field and tearfully embraces his friend. Here is something deep and closely kin to life.

Whether your friend loans you five dollars or saves your life, it is a refreshing experience because it gives you a glimpse into the sanctuary of life.

A friend is somebody to depend on. A little boy depends on his parents. He is always with them. They provide for his needs. But one day the little boy starts to school, and he's in another world. Much of the day is away from his parents. He feels very lonely and may go back to an earlier period when he received attention by crying. But now he is in a new world where this kind of behavior does not work anymore. The little boy begins to wonder what life is all about. He is never really happy in this new world until he finds a friend. Once he finds a buddy he is well on his way to learning what life is all about. But if by the time the boy is twelve, he has not made a friend, he very likely never will.

This is perhaps why baseball was so important to you. Look what someone did for you with a baseball. You lacked confidence in yourself. You could not make friends because of this. You were afraid that you would do or say the wrong thing, so you didn't try. You could not depend on yourself, so you were afraid to depend on a friend. Without interdependence there is no friendship. You might have gone through your whole life this way. But with a baseball and God's help someone planted in you the seed of self-confidence that God watered and grew into the flower of friendship.

You could not get along with others. At school and at play you were miserable because of your inability to get along. With a baseball and God's help someone taught you the spirit of teamwork. You learned that it takes nine boys (or nine girls), to make a team. After this it is easy to learn that it takes many people to make a world. With a baseball someone taught you that no one is ever good enough to criticize another person's error. After this it is easy for you to learn what Emerson meant when he said, "I keep a fair-sized cemetery in the back of my mind in which I bury the faults of my friends."

You could not control your temper. You built up to a level of interpersonal relationships only to shatter it all with one hot burst of temper. This might have plagued your entire life. But with a baseball someone taught you to respect the umpire's decision and to control your emotions. Someone taught you how to make a friend and this was your first lesson in life. For God made friends to tell us what life is all about.

And then God made friends to remind us of himself. A friend is the best thing that can happen to anyone. There seems to be a spark of God himself in friendship and indeed there is. The best in human relations ought to remind us of God. For what goodness we can find in ourselves and in our friends certainly does exist in God. If there is a spark of divinity in friendship, then there must be a fire from which it comes.

David's deep friendship with Jonathan was a factor in his great sensitivity to God's heart. What David found in the heart of his friend he knew must exist to a greater degree in the heart of God. David could never have become the man after God's own heart had he not first learned the lesson of friendship. When you find a friend "that sticketh closer than a brother," you are well on your way to the heart chamber of God. God made friends to remind us of himself.

But this parable is supposed to be about prayer. So what do friends teach us about prayer? Very much, indeed! If a sleepy-eyed neighbor will hear our petition at midnight, surely he who slumbers not nor sleeps will hear our prayers at noon. If a father will give bread to his boy, surely God will give ear to the needs of his children. But a father cannot give bread to a prodigal son in a far country, nor can God grant your requests unless you go to him. So you must go to God. In the cold stillness of the midnight hour you must knock upon the gate of heaven. In the white heat of noon you must storm the citadel of God. In the dark shadows of dusk you must pound upon the doors of eternity. "Ask, and it shall be given you; seek, and ye shall find; knock, and it shall be opened unto you" (Luke 11:9 KJV). This is what our friends have taught us. This is what friends are for. And this is why we sing:

> What a Friend we have in Jesus,
> All our sins and griefs to bear!
> What a privilege to carry
> Everything to God in prayer!

Only when Jane and John seek friends in the community of hope, will they find the fullness of life they want and deserve. "Forsaking all others" in the marriage vows doesn't mean that you give up your friends. Jesus teaches that his disciples are people who ask and seek and knock. They ultimately ask and seek from their heavenly Father. This is their ultimate hope. A preliminary hope is exercised when we knock on our neighbor's door at midnight.

Jane and John find this hard to do. Romanticism tells them they don't need their neighbors. They need only each other. But it is also hard for them to turn outward because they have been indoorized.

Indoorization began with the advent of *liquid fuel heating.* In the days before fuel oil and insulated walls we could not really alter indoor temperature from that outdoors. No one was saying, "Shut the door. You'll let the heat out." After liquid fuel heating, everything was different. When we closed our doors in the winter months, we limited our socialization.

Jane and John were shut in until spring. Areas of socialization, such as the sidewalk, the village square, and the city park were devoid of people.

The second stage of indoorization was *television*. When we piped entertainment into the living room, Jane and John turned in on themselves. A limited amount of socialization happens when we stand in line to buy a ticket at the movie. Even that is gone today for Jane and John if they are over thirty. Only young people go to the movies.

Indoorization was complete when we *shut our doors and windows in the summer*. Jane and John live in air-conditioned cloisters. Socialization was easier when we could go next door and shout through Jim's screen door, "What are you doing, old buddy?" Today we have to push a button which activates the ringing of a bell, and we have to leave our own air-conditioned cloister to get to that button.

The uninvited guest doesn't happen anymore in suburban America. Jane and John have been turned in on themselves. Jesus says we must learn to turn outward.

7

The Community of Hope Is the Church

It is impossible for Jane and John to turn outward, unless they enter community. This is the basic problem in marital life today. There has been an explosion of expectations. Jane and John want all of their expectations met, and they try to meet them in each other. Jane expects John to fulfill her needs for community and to do it by himself. John has the same unrealistic expectation. Jane and John are asking the impossible. When they don't get it, they turn inward without faith, and things go from bad to worse.

Jane and John cannot find community by turning inward; they must turn outward. But no one has told them about community. The commercials they watch on television show groups of happy people drinking beer, but they don't say anything explicit about the communal. They may imply that community is found at the bar. Jane and John, for the most part, don't believe this message. But they don't know where to turn.

I am suggesting that they turn outward to the church. The

church is not the only valid community in the United States. The Jewish synagogue has a beautiful focus which is communal. There are others, but the church is my community, and I choose to write about it.

I make four assumptions about community:

First, community is the gift of the Spirit. The Spirit is like the wind (*see* John 3:8). Wind and spirit are translations of the same Greek word, *pneuma. Pneuma* is from *pneo* which means "to breathe." Pneumonia is a breathing problem and hence the reason we spell the word with a silent *p.* The Spirit blows when he wants to and where he wants to. He also creates community where and when he wants to. Our task is to avoid creating those conditions which make the work of the Spirit impossible. We must wait on the Spirit. We must avoid quenching the Spirit.

Second, a community cannot exist composed of highly fused couples. Community presupposes that all members commune with each other. Fused couples commune only with each other. That is the nature of fusion.

Fused marriages are very much like the churches of my childhood. There were some churches that practiced closed communion. This meant that Baptists would commune only with Baptists and Methodists only with Methodists. There were some churches which practiced closed, *closed* communion, which meant that they wouldn't take communion with anyone other than the members of their own local church. Marriages today are closed, closed communion. Emotional involvement with anyone other than spouse has become taboo. Jane and John don't commune with anyone except Jane and John. The institution of marriage has become a closed corporation with only two members, and their involvement is mutually exclusive.

Not only are marriages closed corporations; they are also located in nuclear families. The institution of marriage is suffocating because of closed, closed communion and it gets very little help from the family because there are only three or four people in it. Families are tight little circles of security. We have been carefully conditioned to live this way. I believe that Daddy and Mommy and Baby is not a functional family. Children can develop better when they can relate to more than two adults. Uncles and aunts and grandparents serve a vital function in the family structure, but these adults are seldom present in a nuclear family.

Three or four people have a relatively narrow repertoire of possible interactions. Eight to twelve people have a much broader possible repertoire. For example, I would not lead a marathon encounter group with only three or four people in it. If only three or four signed up, I would cancel the whole thing. I want eight to twelve people because it's more exciting and more informative.

For thousands of years the human species functioned in groups of more than two adult people, because one man and his wife could not kill a big animal and bring it home by themselves. Survival forced the human species into groups, and I believe this long experience is recorded in our bones. I believe emotional survival will force us to enter community to meet our human needs.

When there is only one significant adult in one's life, one is gambling that he or she dies first. If one loses that bet and one's spouse dies first, one's life is ruined. Death is devastating to the remaining partner. Mobility and other factors make it impossible to go back to the extended family of the past. What does one do? One must break out of the narrow confines of the nuclear family and travel a road that will enlarge the number of one's significant relationships with others. I find this expanded significant group within the body of believers called the church.

If a church is a collection of couples and families, it is not a community. It is a religious club. How can you as an individual tell if a church is a community? It isn't easy, but look for certain prerequisites and ask certain questions:

1. Are singles accepted in the membership and active in the leadership of the church? If singles are segregated into a separate sphere of activity, and if they have no leadership role in the church at large, be skeptical.
2. Is the pastor of the church judgmental in tone or content when he talks about divorced people? A real community recognizes that it needs singles and will actively recruit them. It will not be judgmental. If the church is judgmental, it is probably not a community.
3. Is the social life of the church restricted to couples or segregated between couples and singles? True communities do not practice segregation in any form.
4. Are elderly people active in all phases of the church life? A community is a place where one can grow old with dignity and meaning. If elderly people are patronized, it is not community.
5. Do people describe the church as a place where "blood runs thick?" If blood relationships are of great importance, the church may be a tribe, but it is not a community. Community is a bonding of people which transcends biological kinship.

Third, I assume that the community par excellence is the itinerant band. Jesus came to show us many truths. One of these is what community looks like. In many ways that ragtag band of fishermen which wandered around Palestine is beyond us. I believe, however, we should hold it up as the ideal. I believe it is the yardstick with which we should measure the degree of community which we have in our churches. We enter community as singles and not as couples, because that is the way Jesus invited his disciples to follow him. We make fellowship of members more important than ownership of property, because that is what Jesus did. We focus on the kingdom and not coupledom, because that is what Jesus did. We focus on the eternal more than the ephemeral, because the Master taught us to. We are not afraid to look prophetically at ourselves because Jesus was a prophet. The following story is in a prophetic mode.

The Parable of the Unpopular Sermon

The Westminster Church in Martinsville was a beautiful rustic reason for a small group of people to get together in one place at the same time every Sunday morning. The congregation was composed of retired businessmen and rich women. They were very much "at ease in Zion," a biblical expression that means don't rock the boat for anything, not even if the thing is sinking. If you are going down, do it gracefully with as little fuss as possible. Sinking with class is better than surviving with ambiguity. It was obvious that Westminster had been going down for a long time, but the congregation had kept busy enough with shuffleboard not to notice that the ship was sinking. The sweet, gentle people at Westminster claimed to be in the Christian tradition, but they had put some distance between themselves and that itinerant band that roamed the countryside of Judea, laughing and loving and tearing down ancient institutions. Jesus would have been hard-pressed to get the people at Westminster to so much as leave the county much less dismantle an old and venerable institution.

The Reverend John P. Whitworth was the new pastor at Westminster. He was a tall, raw-boned kind of man and in many ways very unclerical. His sermons during his first month had been innocent enough, and the congregation had no reason to believe that on this first Sunday in Advent he would do anything other than usher Jesus into Jerusalem. No one anticipated that he might try to bring Jesus into Martinsville. This town had its own institutions, and they had done well without Jesus for a long time. The most sacred of them all was the institution of marriage. It could be entered only through the door of romantic love,

and once in, the door slammed shut and all avenues of approach
were blown up and all connecting bridges were burned down.
The Westminster wedding ceremony required the bride and
groom to take a vow that they would forsake all others and cling
only to their spouse. This was the mortar which held the family
together in Martinsville. The existence of these tight little circles
of security fed the economy of the town. There was no room for
Jesus and his itinerant band in the Martinsville marketplace,
nor was there any room for him at Westminster. John P. Whitworth was fresh out of seminary, and he didn't know this.

Just before his sermon, Mr. Whitworth read an additional
passage of Scripture that seemed to have no relationship to
Advent.

> The same day came to him the Sadducees, which say that
> there is no resurrection, and asked him, Saying, Master,
> Moses said, If a man die, having no children, his brother shall
> marry his wife, and raise up seed unto his brother. Now there
> were with us seven brethren: and the first, when he had
> married a wife, deceased, and, having no issue, left his wife
> unto his brother. Likewise the second also and the third unto
> the seventh. And last of all the woman died also. Therefore in
> the resurrection whose wife shall she be of the seven? for they
> all had her. Jesus answered and said unto them, Ye do err, not
> knowing the scriptures, nor the power of God. For in the
> resurrection they neither marry, nor are given in marriage,
> but are as the angels of God in heaven (Matt. 22:23–30 KJV).

But the congregation was not greatly disturbed by this irreg-
ularity. They all knew the passage of Scripture was there, buried
in the last chapters of Matthew's Gospel. Besides, what people
did in heaven was of no consequence in Martinsville or Westminster. If Jesus wanted the angels to run around as sexless
eunuchs, okay, that was his prerogative—just don't mess with
Martinsville. Mr. Whitworth started messing when he read an
additional passage.

> Martha saith unto him, I know that he shall rise again in the resurrection at the last day.
>
> Jesus said unto her, I am the resurrection, and the life: he that believeth in me, though he were dead, yet shall he live (John 11:24–26 KJV).

Whitworth began his sermon by saying that Advent was a season of preparation for the coming of Jesus and that there were institutions in Martinsville that were blocking his entrance. He suggested that it would be exciting if the people at Westminster would try to remove the roadblocks and let the master come in. "We have many assumptions," he said. "One of these is that the most important relationship in life is that of marriage. We are very much like the Sadducees who didn't believe in life after death but believed very strongly in the marriage bond. Jesus encountered the Sadducees with the concept that being 'in the resurrection' was more important than being 'in love' or 'in marriage' and from his conversation with Martha at the death of her brother we know that being 'in the resurrection' is a present reality and not some future hope."

Whitworth continued that though Westminster was for all practical purposes dead, the church could come to life if the membership would come to believe that their relationship with God was as important as their relationship to their spouses. At this point there was an unusual attentiveness in the congregation. Whitworth might have survived the firestorm that followed had he quit here, but he didn't.

"I love my wife very much," he said. "But my relationship with Mary is most ephemeral. It could end tomorrow with either her death or mine. It could end next year in a divorce. Wives don't last forever, and life would be boring if they did. And if I live with Mary forty years on earth, I don't want to continue the relationship in heaven. Too much of even a good thing can get boring." There was a deathly silence in the congregation.

"Mary and I have agreed that we will not forsake all others. We want to be deeply, intimately involved with each member of this congregation, and we would like to start by sharing our Christmas this year with you. We want to suggest that this year the thirteen families of this congregation put up a tree in the parish hall. We suggest we all put presents underneath it for each other and on Christmas morning we open our presents here as well as at home."

At this point two of the elders got up and walked out. Whitworth continued his sermon, even though the response from the congregation was most negative. The next morning he received a call from the bishop. His superior in the faith was furious, "Young man, I received six calls from the nineteen people who attended your service yesterday. They all agreed that you attacked the home, put down marriage, and wanted to do away with Christmas."

"Sir, I suggested that we put Christ first."

"You can put Christ anyplace you want to, but you can't attack marriage and the family."

"My ordination vows require me to drive away from the church doctrines contrary to God's Word, and this is what I am trying to do."

"Who are you to tell me what ordination means? It means that you obey your bishop. Is that clear?"

"Yes, sir," Whitworth answered in a tone that would have been more appropriate for a commanding general than a father in God.

"And don't let me hear any more suggestions about opening presents at church instead of the home," the bishop demanded. "I think you and Mary are having marriage problems, and I want you to see Dr. Allen at Covington tomorrow morning."

"Mary and I have no marriage problem. We have a beautiful, open, and honest relationship."

"I don't care what kind of relationship you have, I want you to get professional help tomorrow."

"I can't afford to see a psychiatrist."

"That's your problem. I have made the appointment, and I expect you to keep it." The bishop hung up.

The next day Reverend and Mrs. John P. Whitworth drove to Covington for marriage counseling. They remained in counseling for three months, and Dr. Allen felt very good about giving reduced rates to the young minister and his wife.

Fourth, I assume that the church for all its imperfection has the best chance of creating an environment where the Spirit may choose to bring community. The church has the heritage and tradition to receive community.

There can be no community apart from a common historical remembrance. A therapy group may do exciting, affirming things, but it is missing remembrance. It cannot be community. In church we must say to each other and to our children, "What mean these stones?" We must make the history of Israel and the history of the church live again. Religious education is prerequisite to community.

Remembrance must be prophetic and not nostalgic. Nostalgia remembers the past, but it remembers selectively. It remembers carefully. It avoids the recollection of anything which would disturb the status quo of the present. Prophetic remembrance is more honest and less selective. It remembers *all*—the good times and the bad. Prophecy remembers our past mistakes and the price we paid for them. Community requires this kind of remembrance.

It also requires a common existential struggle. The struggle to pay for the new church building doesn't count. Community never centers around an edifice. It centers around the work of the Spirit in binding a group of divergent people together. Community is turning outward collectively, outward to pain and oppression and fear.

Community can happen only when a group of people have a common future hope. The history of the work of the Spirit points toward the apocalyptic in the true sense of the word. "Come, Lord Jesus!" is the cry of community. The Christian community recognizes the pain of the present, but it has a communal conviction that this is God's world and that God owns the future.

All is not well in Camelot. There is pain and divorce and disease, and there is little community. The extent to which people are missing community in their lives is the degree to which they will become romantic in their marriage model or child-centered in their families. Child-centered families are living on borrowed time. When the children leave, the family must go through a painful restructuring. If they don't leave, they must create havoc to justify their staying. A child-centered family is a dysfunctional institution.

Parents do a lot of dumb things, but they don't do dumb things for the fun of it. They do dumb things because they are desperate. The church needs to address this desperation.

One of the most human stories in all Scripture is the return of Joseph and Mary from Jerusalem. Halfway home to Nazareth they checked to see if Jesus was in the caravan. He wasn't. In total perplexity the Jewish couple returned to the Holy City and after a long search found their first born in a seminar at the temple.

The lad was only twelve. In many American communities Joseph and Mary could be prosecuted for child neglect. Why didn't Mary check sooner to see if Jesus was with them? Mary was a good mother. How could she overlook such a basic parental obligation? No American mother would have made this kind of mistake. Why did Mary make it?

It was a caravan that left Jerusalem for Nazareth. There was a sense of community in the caravan. Mary could count on the community to help her in the care and nurturing of Jesus. Jane and John don't have this. It is the task of the church to see that they get it.

Jane and John are desperate for community. They need to turn outward with a mission. They have turned inward with romanticism, and they have suffered the bitter dregs of their dyadic exclusivity. If the church fails to provide this mission, it fails to be the church.

The mission of the church is to preach the Word and to administer the sacraments. Jane and John need both Word and sacrament. They need the Word to confront them in their romanticism, as the pre-exilic prophets confronted Israel in its legalism and cultic self-centeredness. But the Word alone is not enough. The Word alone pushes Jane and John toward a judgmental stance, and nothing is so critical as a couple in the posture of piety. Avoid this kind of couple like the rear rotary of a helicopter.

Jane and John need the sacraments. They need to be baptized into the body of Christ and they need to commune with their brothers and sisters in the faith. They need to be sacrificed out of their romanticism into something holy and acceptable unto God. Our experience is that if Jane and John have only the sacrament, they will become superstitious. They also need the prophetic Word. All healing comes from the eternal God who has chosen to mediate it through the grace of the sacramental and the wrath of the prophetic word. The wind of the sacramental and the fire of prophecy are held in the hand of the Holy One. They who would be whole again must feel the immanence of that wind and the judgment of that fire. Those who would peddle healing from any other source have not seen the fountainhead from which healing waters flow.

I find hope in that inner circle of the saints of God where all is forgiven and where all is accepted. Hope is not something we earn. We don't purchase it with good deeds or church pledges. Hope is a gift of God to those who choose to get involved with their brothers and sisters in Christ. Hope is an inner assurance that when we die a part of our friends will go with us. Hope is a sure conviction that when we live, our friends in the faith will not desert us. Hope is believing that come life, come death, *nothing* can separate us from the love of God and from each other. Hope is believing that when we go home, we will go home with our friends. Hope is believing that when we get there, God will receive us with open arms.

Part 3

Parenting
with Love

8

Love Deals Lovingly with Differences

The Song of Solomon begins with a passionate request: *Kiss me for your love is better than wine.* It doesn't say that wine is bad. It just says that love is better. The song sings with explicit passion. It explodes with the joy of relational love. It exudes a deep heart-rendering intimacy.

If there is anything we need today, it is intimacy. The opposite of intimacy is anonymity, a faceless existence, and the cities are full of it. No one knows anyone. People don't have faces. We pass each other at sixty miles an hour, and you can't see the contours of a face at that speed. We don't have neighbors in suburbia anymore. We don't even use the word. We don't talk about our neighbors; we talk about the people next door. There are fewer sidewalks in suburbia. Sidewalks are for intimacy, for casual strolls where you talk to your neighbors and wave at your friends. In some places they don't build sidewalks anymore. They build streets and superhighways for rapid transportation. While we get where we are going quickly, we know few people really well. There seems to be something wrong in sharing a very small part of this planet with a group of people and living in such a way that the structure of the community itself hinders intimacy.

There is no greater contrast to suburbia than the Song of Solomon; it is the most intimate book in the Bible. There is no deep theology, no panoramic sweep of history, just the breathless excitement of a love relationship between two people.

It is not surprising that the Song is one of the most popular books in the Bible. Many of the best known phrases in the English language find their origin here:

A lily of the valleys (2:1)

And his Banner over me was Love (4:1)

A rose of Sharon (2:1)

The voice of the turtledove (2:12)

The little foxes that spoil the vineyards (2:15)

Love is strong as death (8:6)

The book focuses on a love relationship. There are two speakers, and they revel in their passionate love for each other. They explore with tender touch the physical bodies of each other. Their metaphors burst with excitement. A myth about the book is that the couple was Rock Hudson and Doris Day. There is no reason to believe that this Jewish couple in Northern Israel was anymore attractive than the average American couple. They were different from the typical couple in one way: they knew how to love. Listen to them talk in the Song of Solomon:

Your voice is sweet (2:14).

Your face is comely (2:14).

Your eyes are doves (1:15; 4:1).

Your lips are like a scarlet thread (4:3).

Your mouth is lovely (4:3).

You are all fair, my love (4:7).

These people knew how to love passionately, and they have taught us much about it.

They have taught us much about love, but they haven't taught us how to deal with differences. To learn the latter, we must look to the apostle Paul and to the psychotherapist Carl Jung.

Opposites attract. We choose mates who are different from ourselves. We marry people whom we hope will compensate for our inadequacies. John is introverted. He picks Jane for a wife, because she is extroverted. Opposites attract. Over the years this opposition becomes a burden. If you ask Jane and John whether or not they entertain guests at home, you will get two different answers.

John says, "All the time."

Jane says, "Never."

The reality of what we see is colored by the glasses of our different personality types. Jane, who is extroverted, needs much more socializing than her introverted spouse. During their courtship they wanted only each other. Now the honeymoon is over, and the hard part comes—learning to deal lovingly with differences.

Opposites attract. Memories are short. We forget that we chose our spouses because they were so delightfully different from ourselves. After a few years go by (maybe it is seven), we make a fatal assumption. We assume that our spouse's needs are identical to our own. We make what Jung called an unconscious assumption of likeness. John assumes Jane's needs for socializing are no greater than his. Actually, her needs are much greater than his. Extroverts need external validation, and they get it through a large group of friends with whom they socialize. Introverts are better at validating themselves and often need less socializing. Mark Twain said, "Give me a compliment and I'm good for two months." Twain was an introvert. Give me a compliment, and I'm good for twenty minutes. I'm a high extrovert, and like all extroverts I need much external validation. This is not immaturity. It's just the way extroverts are born.

Measurement

How does one identify differences? How does one measure differences? When Jane and John turn inward on themselves, they recognize their differences, but they do it from a judgmental posture.

"John, why don't you like to entertain?" extroverted Jane asks.

"I'm tired. I work all day. When I come home, I just want to rest," introverted John answers.

"Well, is it asking too much to have company once a month?" Jane explodes her frustration.

"We do. We had the Franklyns over just last month."

"John Abernathy, we don't have dinner guests over twice a year!"

"So!"

"So, it is not enough," Jane rebuts.

John is angry now. His face is flushed, "It is never enough!"

"What do you mean by that?" Jane interrogates.

"I can never do enough to please you. If we had guests over three nights a week, it would not be enough. You are insatiable."

Jane and John both become judgmental. They know they have different needs, but they have no way to describe them in a nonjudgmental vocabulary. They must turn to something outside of themselves to measure their differences.

In 1923 Carl Jung, a Swiss psychologist, published in the USA a book about how people are different. He called differences "types." He believed that people are born with different psychological types. Some people are born extroverts, while others are born introverts. People have a different psychological inheritance, just as they have a different biological inheritance.

Jung's theories on type were popular in this country, but there was no simple way to measure one's typology. Two women changed this. Katherine Briggs was a Jungian, and over the years taught her only child, Isabel, the theories of Jung. Between World War I and World War II, Isabel Myers wrote two mystery novels and developed a personality test to measure psychological type (the MBTI, the Myers-Briggs Type Indicator). Her books sold. Her test didn't.

Mrs. Myers wasn't a psychologist, so few people accepted her work. No one would take her test. Finally, her father introduced her to the dean of a medical school. Isabel was able to persuade the dean to give her test to his students. This was the start of the Myers-Briggs Type Indicator, the most popular personality test in the USA today. The success of the MBTI lies in its ability to measure differences and do it nonjudgmentally. You can take an abbreviated version of this test in David Kiersey and Marilyn Bates's book *Please Understand Me* (Prometheus Nemesis, 1978) available at any bookstore. To take the original test, you will have to see a family therapist, or a marriage counselor. (Check the yellow pages for a therapist, and be certain he or she is a member of the American Association for Marriage and Family Therapy.)

It will be a valuable experience for you. One really can't negotiate differences until one can measure them and discuss them nonjudgmentally. Now, for the first time, it is possible to turn inward nonjudgmentally. It is possible to be descriptive about your needs, your spouse's needs, and your children's needs without putting each other down.

Typology

Once you've taken the MBTI, you need to know Jungian typology to understand it. Jung is well known in the United States for his concept of extroversion and introversion, but he is often misunderstood. Extroverts are often thought of as people who like people and are socially adept. Introverts are thought to be the opposite. Introverts are often considered inferior to extroverts.

This interpretation is foreign to Jung, who was himself an introvert. Extroverts are people, who given the option between thinking out loud or thinking to themselves, will choose to think out loud. My extroversion is so high I need to talk out loud to do simple arithmetic. Introverts prefer to think to themselves.

This simple difference between people causes untold unnecessary problems. The problem is because we assume other people to be just like us. Extroverted schoolteachers assume their students are also extroverted when in fact at least a fourth of them are introverted. (Studies indicate that 25 percent of the general population in the USA is introverted. ["Jung's Psychological Types," *Journal of Analytical Psychology*, Vol. 9, pp. 129–135. Broadway, Kansas: Tavistock Publishers, 1964.]). The extroverted fifth-grade schoolteacher asks Johnny a question. She assumes he is extroverted and can "think off the top of his head" just like she can. Johnny is introverted and needs five or six seconds to think about a question before he answers it. Johnny is "slow" answering. His teacher assumes he doesn't know the answer and goes on to someone else for the answer. Johnny knows the answer, but he needs a few seconds to process it internally before he articulates externally. If Johnny's teacher is aware of this, she can train herself to count off five seconds before she expects Johnny to reply to her question.

If you are different from your spouse, you need to make a similar allowance for each other. Extroverts get impatient with introverts for being slow in social interactions. Extroverts need to slow down their communication with their introverted spouses to give them time to process internally. In therapy I have often observed an extroverted spouse introduce a second topic before their introverted mate has had time to process the first. When this happens, the introverted spouse will give up and withdraw. If your spouse is introverted, observe the muscles in his or her face when they are processing internally. Give them time to process before you expect a reply.

Introverts have a responsibility also. They seldom "talk off the top of their head." They usually mean what they say, because they have thought about it first. They assume everyone else does likewise. Introverts must realize their extroverted spouses don't always mean what they say. They may be thinking out loud and "trying something on for size." Introverts often take their extroverted spouses too seriously too soon. They need to learn to ask, "Do you really mean that or are you just thinking out loud?" Learning to recognize and accept differences will save you both pain and misunderstanding in your marriage.

We can avoid much anxiety in our parenting if we accept the fact that our children are different from us. My first family-therapy internship was in Los Angeles. I had to move my family from Massachusetts, which involved a school change for Donna, my second-grade daughter. I felt guilty about this. To atone for my sin, I would pick her up after school each afternoon. I would park in front of the Ivanhoe School in the Hollywood section of Los Angeles, and watch the boys and girls come out the front door. Most of them would come out in groups of two or three. Without fail, Donna would come out by herself. I thought I had ruined her. I knew I would not come out of school by myself. I always had a covey of friends around me. I failed to understand that my introverted daughter didn't need a constant group of people around her.

When Donna was eleven, she wanted to have one—or at most, two—good friends. If she broke up with her "best" friend, it was traumatic. I had a long talk with her. "Look, Donna, if you have five or six good friends and lose one, then it isn't so bad." I wondered why Donna couldn't understand this. As usual, I was projecting my extroversion onto her. Extroverts need five or six good friends. Introverts seldom have more than one or two.

Jung teaches that some people are *intuitive* types and others are *sensing* types. While extroversion and introversion types are well known in this country, intuitive and sensing types are not. Intuitive types are people who see life as a series of relationships. Sensing types are more concerned with facts. Intuitive types are interested in possibilities. Sensing types are interested in actualities. This is really two different ways to see the world. Sensing types are acutely aware of the external environment in which they find themselves; intuitive types are acutely aware of the human relationships in which they find themselves.

I am a map collector and have the walls of my office covered with huge maps and nautical charts. Sensing people notice them. Intuitive people walk into my office and never know the maps are there. Intuitive folk are so preoccupied with their relationship to me that they don't see the maps. If you were to ask an intuitive person five minutes after he or she left my office what was on the walls, that person couldn't tell you!

If the two types were standing on a pier waiting for a sailboat lost in the fog, their response on seeing it would be different. The intuitive type would say, "Ah, there's the boat." The boat now has a new relationship with the pier. It has a visual relationship, and this is what excites intuitive types. The sensing type would say, "It's not here yet." The fact that the boat has not yet arrived is what captures the attention of sensing types.

If you and your spouse are different on sensing and intuition, you need to be aware of it. If you and your child are different on this preference, you need to know it. It will color how you perceive the world in which you live. If the two of you are seeing the same experience, the same facts, the same situation differently—and don't know it—you are flying blind in a relational arena where it is important to see the landing lights. Don't fly blind. What you don't know in your family *will* hurt you. Family life is hard enough when you are aware of your differences. It is impossible when you aren't.

When you know how you are different and when you have a vocabulary to describe these differences nonjudgmentally, you have a better chance of making your family work.

A third way you, your spouse, and your children may be different is in *thinking* and *feeling.* Thinking types are logical in their decision-making process. Feeling types are more value-oriented. I am a high-feeling type and make most of my decisions based on a value orientation. Sometimes this causes me problems. I especially have problems when I am shopping for big-ticket items like automobiles. A few years ago I bought a foreign diesel-powered car. It was a mistake. The car has not performed well. I have had constant trouble with it.

I bought it because I'm a feeling type. I lived in the Panama Canal Zone for three years. While there I bought a sailboat, a Morgan 33 Out Islander. I made the purchase in

Florida and sailed the boat back to Panama. I had never sailed before. My partner had sailed very little. When we were caught in our first storm, we took down the sails and turned on our auxiliary diesel engine. We depended on it to get us out of the storm. It did. It was a Volvo diesel engine.

I promised myself if I ever got back to the States, I would buy that diesel car. I did return, and I did buy it. I bought it out of loyalty. I felt I owed something to the people who made such a fine motor for my sailboat. A week after I bought the car, I was looking at the motor. There printed in the middle of it was:

VOLKSWAGEN—MADE IN GERMANY

The Volvo Company had made marine diesels for years, but at that time it did not make automotive diesels. It was a fourteen-thousand-dollar mistake. A thinking type would not make this kind of mistake. Thinking types would read a consumer magazine and make a more logical purchase.

If you, your spouse, and your child differ on feeling and thinking, be aware of it and learn how to talk about it in a way that is affirming. Thinking types can overlook important family values which enter the decision-making process every day. John, a thinking type, wants to have a gala party on his fortieth birthday. Jane, a high-feeling type, agrees to have a party. Both are excited about the big event. Things go well in their preparation, until they decide whom they are going to invite.

"Well, it's my party, and I want to invite people I enjoy," John says.

"Right, John, you shouldn't have to have people you don't like your birthday party," Jane agrees.

"No political invitations," John pushes his point.

"What do you mean by that?"

"Let's not invite people because we need to," John clarifies.

"Agreed," Jane answers.

"Just people we enjoy."

"Right."

A few days pass, and Jane becomes increasingly restless. "John, do you want to invite the Browns?"

"No, I don't really enjoy the Browns."

"Why not?"

"They're boring."

All of this is logical to John. It is his party. He wants to have fun. *How could anyone fail to see the logic of it?* he asks silently.

"But John, we socialize with the Browns a lot. They've invited us to their house several times."

"I know, but they're not fun people. I don't want them at my party."

"John, I think we should invite them. There will be fifty people at the party. You probably won't even see the Browns except to say hello."

"Listen, Jane, we agreed that it's my party and that we wouldn't invite people for political reasons."

"John, this isn't political. I just don't want the Browns to feel left out," Jane explains. She understands John's logic, but she is struggling with values which go back to her family of origin. She has egalitarian values which say that the whole community is important, and no one should be left out. "John, could we change the rules slightly and invite three or four people for community reasons?"

"I don't understand," John says.

"Well, you invite a couple of people for reasons other than fun and let me do the same."

John hesitates, clasps his hands behind his head and stretches to get more oxygen into his lungs, "That sounds fair enough. Could we expand the list of guests to sixty-five? With that big a crowd, four turkeys wouldn't be so bad."

"Agreed. Sixty-five guests to include four turkeys," Jane echoes.

This is how to negotiate differences. John's logic and Jane's values are both allowed to enter the decision-making process. The end result is a party where they both feel comfortable and a lifestyle that affirms their differences.

The fourth way you and your family members may be different is *judging* and *perceiving.* Judging people need structure in their lives. Judging doesn't mean judgmental, but rather it means that these people like to make judgments in the sense of making decisions. Perceiving people need less structure and are more open-ended. They are comfortable putting off decisions.

John, who is perceiving, and Jane, who is judging, have different needs when they plan a vacation. Jane needs to plan ahead. John needs to be spontaneous. John would like to just drop everything and take off, drive until they get tired and then stop. Drift with the tumbling tumbleweeds. Jane wants every detail planned down to the exact date, itinerary, and leisure activity. No tumbleweeds, please!

Jane, who is a wise woman, plans the vacation a year in advance but doesn't tell John until the day before. "John, sweetheart, why don't we go on a vacation tomorrow?"

"Wonderful, let's do it. Where do you want to go?"

"Oh, it doesn't matter, just let me drive."

Judging parents are often frantic at the lack of decisiveness in their perceiving kids when they, the kids, apply for college. The kids are comfortable in delaying both the decision and the paperwork. Mom and Dad are not comfortable at all.

Workshops

Skill in negotiating differences doesn't come easily. It takes time and practice and guidance. Where do you go for

guidance? The best source is workshops that are being conducted nationwide. The Catholic church has held Marriage
Encounter workshops for both Catholics and non-Catholics
for twenty years. Other churches and counseling centers offer excellent opportunities to work on your family relationships. ACME is an organization which specializes in
marriage enrichment.

I am partial to those workshops which use a Myers-Briggs
format. I have used several approaches to parenting workshops, but none work as well for me as the Jungian. After
everyone has taken the test and knows his or her type, I put
the extroverts on one side of the room and the introverts on
the other. This dramatizes the difference and creates enough
stress to make teaching possible. Then I talk about extroversion and introversion. Next, I divide the class into four
groups: the intuitive-feeling people, the intuitive-thinking
people, the sensing-perceiving people, and the sensing-judging people. Then I give each group the same task:

> Your fifteen-year-old daughter is out on her first date. She
> is supposed to be home at 12 o'clock midnight. She comes in
> at 1:30 A.M. What do you say to her?

This kind of family role play gives each of the four groups
an opportunity to demonstrate their problem-solving style.
But more than that, it creates a setting in which people can
help each other with a common problem. There is power in
people getting together to work on their family problems.
There is healing when people turn outward and focus on
their differences nonjudgmentally. When people do this, they
do more than accept differences; they affirm them.

I spend much time in our workshops teaching parents
how to determine the psychological type of their children.
Children who are ten or older can take the Myers-Briggs

themselves, but younger children would have difficulty reading the questions. Once Mom and Dad know which of the four functions they fall into, I teach them how to determine the functions of their younger children. I follow the interpretation of Kiersey and Bates *(Please Understand Me)* who describe the four functions as:

1. intuitive-feeling types
2. intuitive-thinking types
3. sensing-judging types
4. sensing-perceiving types

I call intuitive-feeling children—*teddy bears*

intuitive-thinking children—*little scientists*

sensing-judging children—*straight arrows*

sensing-perceiving children—*rompers*

Teddy bears are kids who live to relate. Mom and Dad can best motivate them by showing them a relational payoff. "Susie, if you practice your flute, you'll be good enough to go on trips with the band and have lots of fun with the boys and girls." You discipline teddy bears by frowning. If there is a temporary break in the parent-child relationship, control is established.

Little scientists live to improve. They drive Mom and Dad to distraction with endless questions. They are born in the interrogative mode. They make up a tenth of the general population, so there is usually only one or two in each classroom. They know that they are different and often feel lonely. Once they understand something—and it doesn't take them long—they get bored with it. Mom and Dad see them as ungrateful. They lose interest in toys quickly. Schoolteachers see them as "know-it-alls." Such kids may seem arrogant when they really don't intend to be. Little scientists are motivated by rewarding their curiosity. They need affirmation at home. They get little at school. They do well in college but elementary grades are often a struggle.

Straight arrows live to belong. Look at the first day of any kindergarten class. You will see a third of the kids busy learning what they are supposed to do. They love to be line leaders and selected to clean the erasers. Schools were made for straight-arrow children. They usually do well on the conduct side of the report card. You both motivate and discipline these children with rewards and punishments. They like gold stars and they respond well to spankings (open-hand slaps on their little bottoms). Little scientists should never be spanked. They consider it a violation of their bodies.

Rompers live to function. Their favorite part of school is recess. They learn "hands on" and for the present. They refuse to practice for some future payoff. Teachers can motivate straight arrows by saying, "Learn this because you will need it next year in the sixth grade." This won't motivate rompers. They don't think beyond today. The only way you can get a romper to learn Shakespeare is to say, "Tom, we're going to put on Macbeth this afternoon, and you have the lead role." Rompers love to perform and compete. You motivate them by giving them the opportunity to compete. You discipline them by removing them from their peers.

If you want to motivate a straight arrow to build a chair you simply say, "Tom, we are short one chair. Would you build one for us?" This won't work with little scientists. With them you need to say, "Charles, in this class chairs have been built the same way for fifty years. I bet if you really tried, you could come up with a better-designed chair."

If you want to motivate teddy bear Susie, you would be better off saying, "Susie, Uncle Frank knows a lot about building chairs. I bet if you asked him, he would show you how to build a chair." Susie will build the chair just to get to know Uncle Frank better.

Rompers will not respond favorably to any of these approaches. With rompers, you need to say, "Hey, guys, the sixth-grade boys are going around telling everybody that you fifth-graders are too dumb to build a chair." Your fifth-grade rompers will build an outstanding chair just to show those sixth-graders up.

Jane and John are both straight-arrow parents. They are the salt of the earth, really wonderful people. They have three children. One would think that they would have at least one straight-arrow child. Unfortunately, they didn't.

Their first-born was a daughter. She was a teddy bear. Mom and Dad made what Carl Jung calls an unconscious assumption of likeness. All parents do it. We unconsciously think our children are like us. And since they are like us, they should be motivated by the same process which motivates us. Jane and John assumed their daughter was a straight arrow and would be motivated and disciplined by rewards and punishments. When she wasn't, they were frustrated. Like most parents, they did the best they could but nothing worked.

Jane and John didn't know what to do with their teddy bear daughter. They were still puzzled when their second-born entered the family portrait. Now the parental task really became hard. Their second-born son was a little scientist, the most difficult of all types to parent. Through trial and error Mom and Dad had stumbled on a few things that motivated their teddy bear. They tried this on their son. It didn't work. It only made matters worse. Mom and Dad were climbing the walls of desperation by now.

Why they had a third child is beyond rational belief but they did. Hope springs eternal in the hearts of parents. "Please God, let us in our old age have a straight-arrow child." God didn't. Their third child was a romper. So Mom and Dad, two straight arrow people, have three children all different from themselves and all different from each other.

Their third-born romper son explored every avenue of parental frustration known to Atlanta teenagers. If Mom and Dad had realized that their children were different, and if they had known how to motivate the different types, they could have detoured around many miles of painful parenting. Unfortunately they did not know how to deal lovingly with differences.

The best affirmation of differences ever written is chapter 12 of Paul's first letter to Corinth. Paul speaks about a "variety of gifts." He lists wisdom, knowledge, faith, healing, miracle working, prophecy and speaking in tongues as gifts of the Spirit. He uses of the anatomy of the human body to affirm differences. He talks about the interrelationship of feet, hands, ears, eyes, and the human head. Paul belabors the point of human differences.

Paul knows that only when we affirm our differences can we celebrate our union in the body of Christ. The same is true for Jane and John. They must affirm their differences and the differences of their children in a nonjudgmental vocabulary before they can experience the language of love.

Faith looks inward. Hope looks outward, but love looks both ways. Love looks to the personal commitment of faith as the foundation of its existence, but it also looks to the superstructure of the community of hope—the church—for a sense of shelter in the storms of life. The issue is not "Will we have family problems?" Everyone has family problems. The issue is which way will we look when they come. Love looks both ways.

The inward look of faith accepts differences because commitment is deeper than differences. The outward look of hope accepts differences, because it knows that unity grows out of diversity. Love deals lovingly with differences because it has the posture of both faith and hope. It looks inward to commitment and outward to community. It takes both commitment and community to make a family work.

Love is caring enough to get involved with the total life of another person. When the other person is your spouse, there are deep rivers to ford and precipitous chasms to cross, but the rewards of the union are beyond words to describe, beyond sounds to articulate, and beyond mortal thoughts to fathom. Love in a marital relationship is the courage to look inward with faith and outward with hope at the same time.

I believe the apostle Paul and Jung are describing two different sides of the same coin. What Jung calls psychological types, Paul calls spiritual gifts. When in chapter thirteen of First Corinthians Paul describes the gifts of faith, hope, and love, he is identifying differing personality types. Paul doesn't develop the differing of gifts to the extent Jung develops the differing of types, but they are both pointing in the same spiritual direction.

Sensing Perceiving people (SP) "rompers" and Sensing Judging people (SJ) "straight arrows" have received from the Spirit the gift of hope, the capacity to look outward to community. Indeed, what makes people SP and SJ is that early on the Spirit gave them hope and they accepted the gift. The Spirit will also give them faith. The issue is: will they accept the gift?

Intuitive Feeling people (NF) "teddy bears" and Intuitive Thinking (NT) "little scientists" have received the gift of faith, the capacity to look inward with commitment. The issue is: will they accept the gift of hope?

When parents have received the gifts of both hope and faith, the Spirit is then able to bestow on them the gift of love, that wonderful capacity to look both ways at the same time. The Spirit desires to give everyone the gift of love, but some folk quench the Spirit. They refuse to accept the gifts of both faith and hope. They make it impossible for the Spirit to do his work, because faith and hope are prerequisite to love.

Frank and Barbara

Love conquers all. You don't believe it? Listen to this case story. "Frank is staying out at night," Barbara said. "He comes in maybe two or three in the morning," the middle-aged woman said. Frank was on parole from Attica, a penitentiary in New York, and Barbara was worried that he would be busted for staying out late.

Frank's nocturnal escapades occurred once a month at most, but Barbara was afraid that he would break parole. She lived with a liquid fear that washed her objectivity aside. Barbara was forty-five, fat, and worried about her fading beauty. "How could it leave me so fast?" she asked over and over. Frank assured her that she was as beautiful as ever, but there wasn't much conviction in his assurances. Barbara wasn't experiencing a mid-life crisis. Her whole life had been a crisis.

She had been "given away" by her mother when she was three. She was raised by an aunt and uncle. There was no love in her life. She was treated as a servant and not allowed to eat at the table with the family. At age five Barbara was required to do heavy housework and was locked on the back-porch when the family went on trips.

About age thirteen, she walked into a bedroom to clean it and saw her uncle in bed with another woman. After this she lost the marginal acceptance she had worked so hard to achieve. Her uncle accused her of stealing and sent her to a reform school where she lived for three years. Upon her release, she got a job as a maid. Apart from prostitution, this was her only paying job.

Frank was forty. He had been orphaned at age five and raised by his grandmother. At ten he was sent to a reform school for stealing. By age sixteen he had been confined to a forestry camp, and by nineteen he had a bad-conduct discharge from the Army. Then followed a series of convictions for assault and armed robbery with a total confinement of twenty years. When I first saw Frank, he had been out of Attica for nine months and was enrolled at New York University.

Frank had been previously married once, Barbara twice. They had five children, three of whom were Barbara's by her first marriage. Frank and Barbara had lived together two years before they were married. Frank left for a five-year sentence two days after they were married. Barbara lived by prostitution. She was good at it and would write Frank about her success in "the world's oldest profession." When other inmates were reading about the kids and the cat, Frank was reading about the men that Barbara was sleeping with. She gave him a detailed description of each one.

Frank's rebuttal to Barbara's epistles of prostitution was to write about his success in the prison-college program. Frank and Barbara were intensely competitive. Trust and tenderness were not marital goals; they were personal threats. They had programmed themselves to compete, not to love. They could not tolerate each other's success or strength. Nothing had disturbed Barbara as much as Frank's passing grades at NYU. The thought of Frank graduating from college was more than Barbara could bear. She tried every way her brilliant mind could conceive to get Frank to drop out of college. Her beauty was fading, but Frank's mind was not.

Frank would not yield. He was competing with his past as well as with Barbara. The only way he knew to escape from the prison pattern of his past was education.

Frank's last conviction had been for armed robbery. What scared him most was his need to steal. One afternoon he had felt a strong compulsion to rob a convenience store. When he told me this, I asked him to role play a conversation in which he talked to the saleswoman. He did. He talked with tenderness and feeling to the woman, and then something strange happened. The scene shifted to the funeral of Frank's mother. He talked to his mom, then he cried for a few minutes.

"How do you feel?" I asked.

"Like I'm standing all alone in a deep hole."

Frank cried again. Then he slowly began to climb out of that hole. It was dramatic at first with much self-affirmation, but most of his ascent back to a loving and caring-life posture was slow and tortured.

Barbara's past was as battle-scarred as Frank's, but she had one thing going for her. She cared enough about Frank to get involved with his total life. This is love, and the healing balm of this love resurrected a caring relationship between herself and Frank.

They worked hard at turning the big guns of their competitiveness on the world and not against each other. They learned to defuse the explosiveness of their power struggle by letting each other dominate in those things he or she knew best. They practiced being tender with each other. They learned that love is something you do in your marriage, not something you feel in your heart. They made a habit of being tender, whether they felt like it or not.

In short, they made love the main event in their marriage. Today, they aren't sweet, passive people—they never will be—but they have a security in their relationship that nothing can destroy. It will survive as long as they live. Their marital bridge will weather any storm.

In the Greek language there are three words all of which

are translated "love" in English. *Eros* is passionate love and the origin of our word "erotic." *Philos* is brotherly love and the origin of our word "philanthropy." *Agape* is the kind of love we are referring to in this book. *Agape* is the word Paul used in his hymn to love in First Corinthians 13. There are no derivatives of *agape* in the English language. One can only wonder why.

Agape is different from *eros* and *philos*. *Eros* is a matter of passion. *Agape* is a matter of purpose. *Philos* is a matter of family love. (Philadelphia means "brotherly love.") *Agape* is a matter of choice. God chooses to love us in our sin and shame when we are in no way lovable. God loves us because of what he is, not because of what we are. *Agape* love is intentional.

Frank and Barbara developed an intentional love. They started each day, intending to love each other. *Agape* doesn't rule out passion and it doesn't negate family love; it goes beyond them. *Eros* looks only inward. *Philos* looks only outward. *Agape* looks both ways. To do this, the love must be intentional. Frank and Barbara had the courage to stay in therapy long enough for their intentional hate to be translated into intentional love.

Love, like the Panama Canal, is an engineering accomplishment. As the canal connects two great oceans, love connects two great currents in human life, faith, and hope.

9

Love Communicates with Power

I wish I knew what to do," the worried mother said, as she looked at the floor. "It's as if he's not my child anymore. There's this wall between us, and I can't get through to him." The forty-year-old woman dabbed tears from her eyes.

"You're trying everything you know, but you're pushing buttons that don't work," I reflected.

"That's right. I used to be able to talk to him, but for the last two years," she stared out the window with a dazed, numbed expression, "nothing seems to work."

"How old is your son?"

"Fifteen."

In my office this kind of dialogue happens every day. Parents are hurting. My clinical experience for the past seventeen years points toward a breakdown in the ability of many parents to communicate with their children.

These parents are, without exception, caring and concerned. They are doing the best they can. They are active in their church and community. By anyone's definition they are good people. For the most part, they have been successful in every other aspect of their lives. They've overcome most of the problems they have faced—but they can't communicate with their children.

It is a difficult time to be a parent. The Germans say, *Kleine kinder, kleine sorge; grosse kinder, grosse sorge!* ("Little children, little problems; big children, big problems.") But the problems seem to get bigger every year. When I was a teenager, I rebelled against the established order by smoking grapevines we gathered in the woods. The grapevines were neither addictive nor illegal. Drugs are!

Parents need guidelines for child care in general and communication in particular. The following "commandments" are really helpful hints which have been honed on the anvil of my experience as a therapist and as a parent of two daughters.

1. Don't talk tense.

Parents live and work under enormous stress. The anxiety load is extreme. The first task of parenting is to learn how to be a friend to oneself. You must learn how to manage your own stress. If you don't, the stress will be passed on to your children. If your children accept the stress, it will push them dangerously close to the breaking point. Most children refuse to accept the transfer of parental stress, and this refusal results in a communications break.

An example of talking tense is parental concern over the "excessive" time teenagers spend on the telephone. "Susie lives on the phone. I mean it is growing out her ear," the frustrated mother says.

"I can tell you are concerned, but I don't understand why," I confess.

"She talks so much she neglects her homework."

"Is she failing?" I inquire.

"No, no. She has a B average, maybe $B+$ but she could make straight A's if she would study half the time she spends on the phone."

I am wondering what is going on inside Mom. We both know that Susie is extroverted and needs the external validation she gets from friends.

I have concluded that Mom is talking tense. People were made for community, but Susie's mom is not meeting her need for community. She goes to church, but an hour a week is not enough. When she hears Susie meeting her community needs over the phone, she becomes tense. Mom's unfulfilled communal needs color how she talks to Susie about "excessive" phone use.

Mom must first meet her needs; then she can objectively critique Susie's time on the phone. Her unfulfilled needs create so much internal stress that effective communication becomes impossible.

I recommend that parents attend one of the many stress-management workshops which are being offered. If none are available, suggest that such a workshop be offered in your church.

2. Don't ask questions.

Children, especially teens, are bombarded with questions. Nothing turns them off quicker or produces less information. "What happened at the party?" will not get results. If your child responds with a shrug, consider that noverbal response the most you can hope for. Now listen to an exercise in frustration:

"Why were you late coming home last night?"

"We drove around after the movie."

"Where did you go?"

"I don't know."

"What do you mean you don't know? Where did you go?"

"Mother, I don't know. We just drove around."

"Listen, am I your mother?"

"Yes."

"Well, why can't you tell me where you went?"

This futile dialogue can go on for an hour, and the only information you are going to get is that your daughter reluctantly agrees that you are her mother.

For a full decade I asked the least productive question in the English language, "What happened today at school?"

"We had recess."

"What else?"

"Nothing."

"What did you have for lunch?"

"Don't remember."

Parents need information about their kids. They need to know what is happening in their lives. Questions that are asked directly in plain, simple English don't work. Life would be easier if questions worked; they simply don't. We must learn to get information in other ways. We must learn to go in the backdoor when the frontdoor of the interrogative is closed.

3. Don't interpret.

Interpreting is alluding to some unseen spirit that hovers over the house. "Mary, in this house we don't drive around after the movie. It just isn't done. Is that clear?" What won't be clear to Mary is the amorphous spirit that dictates what is done "in this house." Children are concerned not only with rules but also with the source of the rules. "Interpreting" keeps kids in the dark. They need to know who makes the rules. In their struggle to gain autonomy and responsibility, children need to push against the "rulemaker." Interpreting prevents this.

4. Express your desires directly.

"Mary, I want you home by twelve o'clock." Children need clear boundaries and explicit guidelines. They need to know that the boundaries come from you, the parent. Parents must be the architects of their own instructions, and they must claim ownership of their own guidelines. Practice putting power into the pronoun *I*. Boundaries need to be set with both firmness and flexibility. There must be flexibility to recognize the personhood of your children. Doing this requires a direct expression of your desires.

5. Express your fears directly.

"Mary, when you are late coming home, I worry about you. I worry about you a lot." Children need to know where their parents are in their emotional posture. As a parent, you have an equal need to communicate your feelings to your kids. Your child may be able to guess some of your feelings, especially your anger, but guesswork isn't good enough. For your own emotional health and that of your children, you need to communicate clearly your anger, hurt, and fear. Practice saying, "I worry." "I am angry." "I am frustrated."

6. Don't be intimidated.

"You're a hypocrite. You smoke. Why can't I?" the angry teenager explodes. The parent feels powerless, hurt, and ashamed. The teen appears to be appealing to fair play but is really pushing the "guilt button." Teenagers will manipulate their parents by playing on parental feelings of guilt, if they can. Teens can "smell" when their parents are unsure and hesitant. Like all people, teens operate upon what they assume to be their self-interest. If a power struggle develops with their seniors, teens will seize an unfair advantage. But a teen cannot gain control unless the parent lets it happen.

Don't be intimidated. "Mary, I smoke because I'm an adult, and because I choose to smoke. When you're an adult, you'll have the same option."

"All the other kids smoke."

"That's not the issue. The issue is that I don't want you to smoke. If you give me reason to believe you're smoking, you'll be restricted to the house for a week."

"That's not fair."

"Fair or not, it's my rule, and I expect you to abide by it."

When Mary launches into an emotional inquiry as to why she can't smoke, it is a teen interrogating her parent. Don't subject yourself to interrogation. Simply end the conversation. If necessary, walk away.

7. Negotiate from strength.

"Mary, I'm willing to discuss what time you come in, but the final say is mine."

Parents need to negotiate boundaries with their older teens, but they must not abdicate the throne of their parental responsibility to do so. Being a parent means making decisions for adolescents. When they are capable of making their decisions, they won't be adolescents. They'll be adults. However, if you want them to develop their own sense of responsibility, you need to negotiate boundaries with them, especially in their late teens.

I had a friend who lived next door to the chief of police. He had sons nineteen and twenty years of age who lived at home. It was an open secret that they were smoking marijuana. He was puzzled as to what he ought to say to them. He could have said, "As long as you live in my house, you will not smoke it." He had a sense that this would alienate them, and he wanted to stay close to them. He knew, however, that his neighbor, the chief of police, would arrest them if he smelled the odor coming from the house.

His solution was this. "I would prefer you not smoke it *at all*, but would you guys agree to not smoke it at home?" They did. This is negotiation, and it recognizes the emerging adulthood of your late teens.

Try to create a setting for discussion with your early teens and a climate of negotiation with your late teens. "Mary, what seems to be an appropriate hour for you to come home on Saturday nights?" Give Mary a chance to make input into your decision-making process. She'll treasure the opportunity and feel better about the final decision that you make.

8. Don't beg.

You give away power when you do. Parents need all the power they have. Children usually have a better support group than their parents. They are in contact with their peers at school and talk frequently about their interactions with their parents. Walk down any high school hallway, and you'll hear some teen say, "Well, my mom. . . ."

Parents don't have this kind of support group. They are often lonely in their role as parents and may feel that no other parents are as impotent as they are. Sometimes they feel desperate and beg their children to obey. Begging doesn't work. It only lowers you in the eyes of your children. It sends a signal to your child that you are desperate. Begging tells your child you have abdicated the throne of parental decision making. A power struggle will inevitably follow between you and your child with regard to who makes the rules.

Never say, "Please." You are better off to say, "Mary, I know you don't like it but I make the rules. That's the way it is."

9. Slow down your communication.

Discuss one topic at a time. Refuse to let your child bring up other topics until you are finished with the first.

"You don't understand," Mary says when Mom is halfway through her first sentence.

"Understand what?" Mom inquires.

"You just don't understand me," Mary says. When this happens, the parent has been diverted to a second topic before he or she has been able to complete the first. You are better off to ignore the diversion effort or to say, "Mary, I'm not trying to understand you right now." Then you should return immediately to your first topic.

Communication is hard enough when one focuses on one idea. It becomes impossible when several ideas are discussed at the same time.

Parents need to receive messages from their children as well as to send them. When your child is trying to communicate with you, follow a two-step process of listening. Once you have a clear picture of what your child is saying, repeat the message back to him or her. Then ask, "Mary, is this what you're saying?" When Mary says you have understood her message, then agree with as much of it as you can. Look for areas in which you can give honest agreement and state it. Always give minimal agreement which is, "Mary, I agree that you feel. . . ."

Conjunctions short-circuit communications. "Mary, I hear what you're saying, but. . . ." The conjunction "but" introduces a new idea too quickly. Remain with Mary's idea, even if it is repugnant to you. Repeat it back verbatim or paraphrase it, until Mary agrees you understand it. Once you have given Mary both understanding and agreement, you are in a better posture to state your own position. This technique won't work when you and Mary are in a heated argument, but in more rational moments it works wondrously well. It also will give you a chance to model good communications for your teen.

10. Share your childhood.

"Mary, when I first started dating, I was scared stiff that I would do or say the wrong thing."

"Really?" your teenager will beam.

The best way to get information from your teen is to share yourself. Teens are interested in knowing how their parents coped with problems similar to their own. But the sharing process requires that you reveal your own teenage fears and uncertainties. If you tell only about your teenage hardships, your children won't listen.

"Dad, I know all about you walking three miles to school in the snow." You must share your inner self.

These "commandments" can improve your ability to send and receive messages without eroding your position as the parental decision maker. However, they must *not* be used at the expense of "economy." Most communication theories fail to consider that parents are busy people and have responsibilities other than nurturing their children.

I have had clients who lost their marriage because they were uneconomical in their communication with their children. Communication is important, but it is not worth your total energies. It's important to send and receive messages with your children, but the whole process must be kept in perspective.

10

Only Love Can Heal

If I speak in the tongues of men and of angels, but have not love, I am a noisy gong or a clanging cymbal. And if I have prophetic powers, and understand all mysteries and all knowledge, and if I have faith, so as to remove mountains, but have not love, I am nothing. If I give away all I have, and if I deliver my body to be burned, but have not love, I gain nothing.

Love is patient and kind; love is not jealous or boastful; it is not arrogant or rude. Love does not insist on its own way; it is not irritable or resentful; it does not rejoice at wrong, but rejoices in the right. Love bears all things, believes all things, hopes all things, endures all things.

Love never ends; as for prophecy, it will pass away; as for tongues, they will cease; as for knowledge, it will pass away. For our knowledge is imperfect and our prophecy is imperfect; but when the perfect comes, the imperfect will pass away. When I was a child, I spoke like a child, I thought like a

173

child, I reasoned like a child; when I became a man, I gave up childish ways. For now we see in a mirror dimly, but then face to face. Now I know in part; then I shall understand fully, even as I have been fully understood. So faith, hope, love abide, these three; but the greatest of these is love (1 Cor. 13).

It was in a small town in northern Mississippi that thirteen-year-old Ted Brothers grew up. He and his younger sister had two overpowering influences in their lives: the cotton fields and their father's church. In the late 40s the farming people of Mississippi ordered their lives around the planting and harvesting of cotton. School started in July and was out the end of August for what was called "cotton picking." In mid-November, when the fields had been picked clean, school started again. Spring was for planting cotton, summer was for chopping, fall was for picking. December was for pulling and what little time was left was for praying for more rain and less boll weevils.

The other influence in Ted Brother's life was his father's church. The human creature, being both gregarious and religious by nature, will congregate somewhere if the existing social institutions will let it. In Mississippi, that institution was the country church. There was preaching Sunday morning and Sunday night. Wednesday night was prayer meeting. Thursday night was church visitation. Friday night was for Sunday-school parties and Training Union rallies. There was always some religious reason to get the farming folk together. The church was the social center of the community. The people had time for nothing but the cotton and the church. Ted Brothers reveled in this way of life. He loved both the fields and the church. He could pick two hundred pounds of cotton a day, and he would gladly give a tenth of his earnings to the church. He picked cotton with the same people he went to church with. There was a laboring and worshiping community that lived together.

A normal childhood would have matured well in this rural setting, but Ted's thirteen years had been stormy. His parents were mismatched. They hated each other with an open hostility. Ted's mother was jealous, and Ted's father was outgoing. It was a marriage that should never have been. Ted knew this and had long talks with his mother. She threatened to leave, and although Ted knew the marriage was unworkable, he begged her not to go. In 1949 in Mississippi, marriages were said to have been made in heaven. Anyone who unmade a marriage was the personal friend and intimate associate of Satan.

Late one October afternoon, Ted came in from the cotton fields. "Where's Mother?" he asked.

"She's gone, gone to Kansas," was the agonizing answer of the lad's father. And the young man broke into tears. The unbearable had happened. Years of marital madness had erupted into the lava of separation, and the separation would slowly simmer into the final funeral of divorce. There was no neat white stone in a patch of green where Ted could grieve over his mother's going. There was no community ritual with which to bury this relationship. The townspeople wanted to know, "Where's your mother?"

"When's she coming back?"

"Did your mom really leave your dad?"

They spoke with tongues, the tongues of men and angels, but they had no love. Some were curious; others were patronizing, but they had no love. They were noisy gongs, clanging cymbals and the cacophony of their chorus assaulted the soul of Ted Brothers. Some of them understood the mystery of divorce, and others were willing to move mountains to help the young man, but they lacked love. The ledger of their lives was balanced with helpfulness, but their hearts were bankrupt for a lack of love.

There were three hundred people who lived in that town, and no one could remember anyone ever getting a divorce. Divorce was something you read about in Memphis—some unpardonable sin of the city. And since life in that rural hamlet was often boring, and since Ted's father was pastor of the local church, the farming folk talked of nothing but the divorce. They were afraid to encounter the preacher with their curiosity, so they focused on the preacher's son.

Ted was suffocated by their questions, embarrassed by their attention, and terrified by their nonverbal communication. It screamed long and loud, "You're untouchable." The young man, who was intensely devout, wondered if anyone cared. Was there any other person who hurt the way he did?

In those days in that community the men and boys would congregate outside before church services began. Frequently, they would not enter the sanctuary until halfway through the first hymn. They would lean against the shade trees and spit tobacco, or they would mull about in some masonic ritual of masculinity. Those who felt that they were the most masculine were always the last to go in.

Ted normally enjoyed this rural religious rite, but this Sunday he could not face his peers. He went inside where the women were. Dazed and depressed, he cowered in the back. An eleven-year-old girl, whose name was Mary Jo, found his fetal retreat. With tones of tenderness, with eyes of warmth and acceptance, she said, "Why don't you go outside where the boys are?" He did. And as he did he felt that Mary Jo cared, that she was really concerned about him as a person.

For a long time this caring was all that young man had to go on. Then one day he came to realize that Mary Jo cared because God cared, and this realization made a difference in his life.

Why did Mary Jo save the young man when all the others failed? Mary Jo was patient and kind. She was not arrogant or rude. She didn't insist on her own way. She did not function by force. She didn't ask questions. She recommended, and Ted followed her recommendation. She suggested, and there was love in her suggestion.

Small towns of the 40s and 50s were notorious for their gossip, and for this reason alone many people sought the freedom of big cities. Small towns were thought to have no redeeming factors. "God made the country, man made the cities, and the devil made the small town," people said. Small-town institutions were so dictatorial in their control that freedom to be one's unique self did not exist, it was said.

Some of this was true, but the evidence is overwhelming that people survived the suffocating controls of country towns and that beautiful relationships did exist. People can survive their institutions, but they must affirm themselves to do it. They must bear all things, believe all things, hope all things, endure all things.

The critical question is "How can we do it?" How can we reaffirm the uniqueness and beauty of people? How can we put people first and institutions second? How can we explode the primacy of people loudly enough that the marketplace will listen and learn? When was the last time a human interaction made you feel that life is basically good and that people are wonderful?

Jesus spent most of his short life answering these questions. The big institution of Jesus' day was not marriage and the family. It was neither the media nor the marketplace. It was the Sabbath. By observing certain customs on the Sabbath day, one felt good about one's self as a person and could work one's way to heaven. Nice, neat. Cut, dried. Just the way the Jews wanted it. But Sabbath-day observance became as oppressive as small-town gossip. The rules and regulations multiplied with madness. If you broke the slightest rule, a dozen bony fingers were pointing you out and pushing you down. Paul put it so well, "When we were childen, we thought like children, we spoke like children, but childhood days are over."

Jesus agreed. On one occasion, Jesus exploded! "Man was not made to serve the Sabbath. The Sabbath was made to serve man" (*see* Mark 2:27). Jesus said, "People are more important than the institution of the Sabbath." The Pharisees, the Sabbath keepers, eventually killed him, but they could not kill his affirmation of the primacy of people. People are primary and precious. Institutions are secondary and subservient. This was the good news that Jesus shouted from the roof tops.

And this was the good news which saved Ted Brothers. There were all kinds of pious people who tried to destroy the young man. The institution keepers were fearful of the father, so they waited in ambush for the son. Getting a divorce was breaking the rules. It was not keeping the Sabbath; somebody had to pay. The preacher's son was it. The God of marriage was angry. A sacrificial lamb must be slaughtered to appease the gods, to save the institution. The preacher's son was it.

But the institution keepers had forgotten how the Father of our Lord Jesus Christ can resurrect love in the eyes of an eleven-year-old girl. If you were to ask Mary Jo if she remembered that day, she wouldn't remember it at all. Strange how the grace of God can flow through us, and we don't even know it. But God knows it. And Ted Brothers knew it, and the institution keepers—well, they are hopeless. They will never learn. But we have a task. We must tell people they are precious. We must show people they are precious. We know that God made people first and institutions second. And if you've had a bad marriage, it doesn't mean you are a second-rate citizen and if you've dropped out of school it doesn't mean that your humanity is in question. These are institutions, and they come second. We are children of God because we were born this way. God made us. God loves us. God redeemed us, and the redeemed of the Lord are precious in his sight.

But what does love mean, and why is love first? Now abideth faith, hope, and love, these three, *but the greatest of these is love.* There were all kinds of faithful folk who could not minister to Ted Brothers because faith is something you do. Faith is dependence on God, and his Son, Jesus Christ. Faith is commitment and it often leads to involvement. Faith restores our severed relationship to God, but faith won't minister to Ted Brothers. Faith gets me right with God, but it won't help Ted.

Hope won't either. Hope looks forward to the future. And we must have confidence in the future to make sense out of the present, but hope won't heal a heartbroken boy. There were many people who said, "Everything's going to be all right," but Ted could not escape his present pain long enough to find solace in some distant future. He was going through a present hell and could not see a future heaven. Hope didn't help, but love did. Only love can heal. Only love can accept. Only love can forgive. Only love in the eyes of an eleven-year-old girl broke through the agony of the young man's heart and made him whole again. And this is why Paul said, "Now abideth faith, hope and love. These three but the greatest of these is love."

Love is the greatest because love looks both ways. It looks inward to the commitment of reconciliation; it looks outward to the community of the concerned where reconciliation is actualized. Only love can heal. The love of God flowed through Mary Jo into Ted Brother's troubled heart, because she looked both ways. She looked inward with faith to a troubled friend; she looked outward with hope to the community where healing could happen. She did it all at once with a very few words, "Why don't you go outside where the boys are?"

Jane and John need this kind of love. In the marital creek that meanders through their relationship, there are endless rocks of personal pain. Feelings are hurt, values are questioned, bills go unpaid, children are sick, birthdays are forgotten. Hurt happens. They need healing. And so do you. You need the brokenness in your life healed. You need your family to work. You don't need to be lonely. You don't need your talents to be wasted. You don't need to be ignored.

Healing can happen in your family, but there must be *faith* and there must be *hope* and there must be *love*. And they must come in that order. The commitment of faith comes first, the outward look of hope to the church comes second, and finally, please God, the spiritual intimacy of love will be poured into your life.